Don't sqveeze de bow!

Alexander Schneider in the 1950's.

Don't

sqveeze

de bow!

Reminiscences about
Alexander Schneider

compiled by
Loren Glickman

TERRA NOVA PRESS
G.B. Manasek, Inc.
Norwich VT 05055-1204
1996

ISBN 0-9649000-3-3

First edition
First printing

iv

Acknowledgment:

A few words of thanks are due.
First, to the ninety–plus people whose reminiscences
make up the whole fabric of this book.
To my former student and hard–working secretary,
Lisa Alexander, who laboriously entered all the letters
into the computer, and who, without audible complaint,
accepted my changes in the order of the material
again,
and again,
and yet again.
To Tom Suárez, who contributed so many photographs.
And finally to my wife, Dobbie Glickman, for being ever
helpful and patient with me throughout the various stages
of bringing this book to light.

Loren Glickman

Introduction:

I met Sasha first in the early fifties when I was a player in an orchestra he conducted at Dumbarton Oaks, Washington. Subsequently he and I performed and recorded concerts of Stravinsky's chamber music, with the composer conducting. Later, Sasha organized the Festival Casals in Puerto Rico, and I became the orchestra contractor. We worked together closely for the next twenty years, developing the festivals in Puerto Rico, concerts at The New School, Carnegie Hall, the parks in New York, recordings at Columbia Records and RCA Victor, and other projects too numerous to mention.

The idea for this book was born shortly after Sasha's passing. Since I remembered so many particular occurences, warm, serious, touching, or downright funny, I thought others who knew him would have similar memories and would want to share them. I put out a call for recollections and anecdotes and they flooded in.

The problem was how to organize these recollections. Should they be chronological? Should they be categorized by project, viz the Festival Casals, personal friends, the NY String Orchestra, chamber music associates, lovers, etc.? In the end, I decided to keep things rather loose and not to worry too much about organization. People who loved Sasha, or responded to his artistry, will be interested in everyone's stories about him.

Another problem was deciding if I should retain some of the more off–color anecdotes. Sasha was a very earthy man, and to totally clean up his act would be to deprive us of a very endearing quality of his personality. Finally, I kept some and omitted some. I hope I haven't offended too many readers, one way or the other.

One final note: I did not attempt to render Sasha's accent into phonetic English. For one thing it would have been impossible — and for another, one would have to hear the actual cadences of his voice to do him justice. We who knew him will inject the accent and vocal quality of our own memories into these anecdotes. Only in the few cases where it seemed crucial, did I attempt the impossible, and wrote "vot" and "loff" to try to give the flavor of his "eccent."

And now, on with the performance.

Loren Glickman
Englewood, NJ

Dramatis personæ

Schneider, Alexander: Our friend and mentor. Does not appear onstage in this performance.

Soloists:

Ansell, Steve: Former member of N.Y. String Seminar

Bairds: The Baird family of Buffalo, friends, music lovers, widely known for their philanthropic activities.

Becerra, June: One of Schneider's friends in San Juan and ardent supporter of Festival Casals

Bergner, Yosi: Good friend in Israel

Bolpata, Ramon C.: Professional cellist. Former member N.Y. String Seminar.

Borer, Jeffrey S., M.D.: One of Schneider's last doctors. Great admirer and music lover.

Brandt, Yanna Kroyt: Daughter of Boris Kroyt, violist with Budapest Quartet. Friend since her childhood.

Brown, Keith: Conductor and trombonist. Faculty, Univ. Indiana. Former member of Casals Festival Orchestra.

Brown, Stephanie: Concert pianist and chamber music artist.

Burns, Stephen: Trumpet soloist. Former member N Y. String Seminar.

Carr, Norman: Violinist. Former member Casals Festival Orchestra.

Ceci, Jesse: Concertmaster of Denver Symphony; former member Casals Festival Orchestra.

Cleveland Quartet: World famous string quartet, formed under Schneider's guidance.

Cohen, Isidore: Violinist formerly with Juilliard Quartet and Beaux Arts Trio, and former concertmaster of Casals Festival Orchestra.

Conant, Robert S.: Concert harpsichord soloist.

Cot, Catherine: Writer. Family friend since childhood.

Dispeker, Thea: Concert manager, old friend.

Forman, Suzanne M.: Music lover.

Frank, Claude: Concert pianist, former student of Schnabel.

Fredrickson, Richard: Double bass artist. Former Casals Festival Orchestra member.

Fremerman, Elana: Violinist, former member of N. Y. String Seminar.

Fukuhara, Mayuki: Violinist, former member of N. Y. String Seminar.

Garbousova, Raya: Famous cello soloist, old friend.

Gearhart, Fritz: Conductor. Former member of Schneider's String Institute, Buffalo.

Gearhart, Pamela K.: Friend. Buffalo, NY.

Gilson, Sheila andStan: Music lovers, concert goers.

Glickman, Loren: Old friend. Chamber music colleague. Schneider's orchestra contractor.

Gottlieb, Marc: Concertmaster, Tulsa Symphony. Former member Casals Festival Orchestra.

Gould, Arlene: Music lover, friend and sometime assistant to Schneider.

Hanson, Marjory: Former secretary at Casals Festival office.

Harrell, Lynn: Solo cellist, former member Casals Festival Orchestra.

Haupt, Charles: Concertmaster, Buffalo Symphony. Former member of Casals Festival Orchestra.

Herz, Gerhard: Administrator with Louisville Chamber Music Society. Old friend.

Hoffman, Robert: String bass player. Former member, N.Y. String Seminar.

Howard, Al: TV producer, former percussionist in Schneider's New York concerts and recordings.

Hutchinson, Henry: Concertmaster, Puerto Rico Symphony. Former member of Casals Festival Orchestra.

Katims, Milton: Conductor, viola soloist, former member New York Piano Quartet with Schneider.

Keesecker, Jeff: Bassoonist, former member of the N.Y. String Seminar.

Kestenbaum, Milton: String bass player. Former member of Casals Festival Orchestra.

King, Molly: Former secretary. Casals Festival office.

Klein, Selma: Music lover, concert goer.

Kristanovich, Dmitry: Former member of N.Y. String Seminar.

Laredo, Ruth: Concert pianist. Old friend.

Lederer, Sidone: Music lover, concert goer.

Lehman, Thelma: Seattle music lover, philanthropist, old friend of Schneider.

Lehr, Catherine: Former member of N.Y. String Seminar.

Lennon, David: Former member of N.Y. String Seminar.

Levick, Mildred & Irving: Old friends and music lovers.

Lilly, Barbara: Former secretary to Schneider.

Long, Sidney: Writer and former book collaborator with Schneider.

Malkin, Anna: Violinist. Former member of N.Y. String Seminar.

Mensch, Homer: Great double bass artist and teacher.

Morel, Rene A.: Violin repairman. Old friend of Schneider.

Neubauer, Ann: Wife of Schneider's former piano technician. Old friend.

Perlman, Itzhak: World famous violin soloist.

Pruzan, Carl: Old friend from Seattle.

Rascusen, Barbara: Sculptor. Old friend from Burlington.

Rampal, Jean-Pierre: World famous flute virtuoso. Colleague.

Reed, Christine: Former secretary. Casals Festival office.

Reinhart, Jinny and Paul: Old friends from California.

Rhodes, Samuel: Violist with Juilliard String Quartet. Chamber music colleague.

Rockmore, Clara Reisenberg: Old friend from childhood.

Rudie, Tina: Music lover and old friend.

Sackson, David: Chamber music violinist. Friend.

Sallar, William: Music lover.

Sanders, Karen Elaine: Violinist. Former member N.Y. String Seminar.

Saslav, Isador: Violin soloist. Professor. Former member Casals Festival Orchestra.

Scelba, Tony: String bass player. Former member Casals Festival Orchestra.

Schneider, Greg: Nephew.

Schulberg, Betsy: Old friend.

Schwarz, Gerard: Conductor of Seattle Symphony. Former member Casals Festival Orchestra.

Seischab, Lisa: Bassoonist. Former member N.Y. String Seminar.

Siegel, Elliot: Violinist. Former member Casals Festival Orchestra.

Smith, Emmy: Old friend. Music lover.

Smith, Reed: Former member of N.Y. String Seminar.

Smukler, Laurie: Violin soloist. Teacher. Former member N.Y. String Seminar.

Sorkin, Herbert: Violinist. Former member Casals Festival Orchestra.

Soyer, David: Cellist. Guraneri String Quartet. Former colleague.

Stern, Isaac: World famous violin soloist. Old friend.

Stewart, Don: Clarinetist. Former student, Marlboro Music School.

Suárez, Thomas: Violinist. Former member N.Y. String Seminar.

Taplin, Frank E.: Old friend. Music lover, philanthropist.

Tsilibes, Alexandra Marie: Former member N.Y. String Seminar.

Tuttle, Karen: Violinist. Former colleague of Schneider in Schneider Quartet.

Wallace, David: Violinist. Former member N.Y. String Seminar.

West, Lilly: Old friend.

White, David: Musician, former student, Marlboro School of Music.

Wincenc, Carol: Flute soloist. Chamber music colleague.

Wolfe, Paul: Conductor. Former member Casals Festival Orchestra.

Woodhams, Richard: Solo oboist, Philadelphia Orchestra.

Xucla, William: Double bassist. Puerto Rico Symphony.

Isaac Stern:

(excerpted from his speech at a memorial for Sasha, April 23, 1993.)

It was difficult to speak earlier, particularly after the very moving and deeply heartfelt remarks by Marta Istomin. Sasha and I are each other's oldest friends. I speak in the present tense because for all of us here, he has not and will not be gone. We met in San Francisco 57 years ago, when I was 15 years old, and we became very close friends almost immediately. And in the intervening decades, he has been and remains the most potent, the most truthful, the most permeating musical influence I have ever had. I don't believe that I think or feel a phrase to this day, or even just think about music, without asking myself: "What would Sasha say? What would he feel?"

All these young people here, and those colleagues of my generation, know to what degree he has — in this part of the 20th century — permeated the sound of music for so many of us... with most of all, his lust for life, his joy of living! Which is why it is fitting that today is not a memorial but a celebration. A celebration where the young here are the continuing thread of "Sasha'sness". It's a wonderful infection. It should be more general throughout the world of music making. And those of us here, gathered together because we love him and we think of him as being in the present, will hopefully be able to carry his torch, each of us with a small candle for him.

Clara Reisenberg Rockmore:

I knew Abrasha since childhood. I came from St. Petersburg where I studied violin with Leopold Auer. When political conditions (in Czarist Russia) became unbearable for Jews in Petersburg, my family moved to Vilna. I was then ten or eleven years old. In Vilna, I met Abrasha, who was just a few years older. My older sister, Nadia Reisenberg, a wonderful pianist, joined a trio with Abrasha and a cellist, and played in a theatre pit for the silent movies of that period. I remember marveling at their "musical agility" as they watched the film and suddenly would begin playing music appropriate to the action on the screen.

Sasha (or Abrasha, as I knew him) was always a very sweet, fun–loving, and considerate boy, and remained the same throughout his life, for we stayed friends all the years of his life. I mourn the loss of my dear friend.

Thea Dispeker:

I knew Sasha practically all my life but have a special recollection of having met him personally in Munich where I grew up, or in Berlin where I lived for 9 years before coming to the United States in the fall of 1938. My family and I knew his first wife and her family. She belonged to a high – class Jewish family in Cologne, playing a prominent role in the music world during the pre–Hitler time.

My first remembrance of meeting Sasha is in the early 1940's. We, of course, had many mutual close friends among musicians and the music establishment in New York and America in general. We became closely connected by practically working together every day, when he, Mrs. Leventritt and Leopold Mannes asked me in 1948 (or 1949?) to become the manager and executive secretary of the first Casals Festival in Prades in the Pyrenees. Sasha visited Casals in Prades where he lived in a tiny little gardener's house of a villa, having left Spain on account of Franco. The purpose of his visit was to persuade Casals to come back and concertize in the United States again. But Casals refused by saying: "I will not set foot on American soil as long as its government will do business with Franco." "Then, I guess,

America has to come to you," Sasha answered. He immediately returned to New York and got hold of numerous well-to-do ladies in New York and other major cities, persuading them to finance a Casals Festival in Prades. Sasha also made arrangements with Goddard Lieberson of Columbia Records to record Casals conducting as well as playing the cello. (The orchestral recordings could not be realized because of the American union.) The orchestra consisted half of Americans and half of Europeans. Sasha was most instrumental by convincing most of the concertmasters and section leaders of our major orchestras to play in this orchestra, even at the last desk, all paying their own transportation and expenses. He also got young musicians such as Isaac Stern and Eugene Istomin to play in the orchestra and for chamber music with Casals. It is also Sasha who got every great soloist of that time from all over the world to come and perform without any remuneration. Among others: Clara Haskil, Dame Myra Hess, Joseph Szigeti, Arthur Grumiaux, Maria Stader, Rudolph Serkin, Paul Tortellier, etc.

The first Festival was in June 1950, rehearsals starting three weeks ahead of time. Sasha was day and night around Casals, organizing the daily rehearsals, and mainly, persuading Casals to record. Casals was terribly afraid of it and gave another excuse every day why he would not be able to record. Sasha, also playing in the orchestra, was the father-confessor and friend of all the musicians, but one day he had a terrific fight with one of them which escalated into a fist fight, and he hit him hard in the face. This incident, of course, created a revolution in the orchestra, but soon it ended by Sasha embracing and kissing his enemy.

Sasha also succeeded by getting the famous "Life" photographers Mili and Bourke-White to Prades, who took pictures during the concerts, even climbing up the columns and walls of the crowded church. The concerts were usually over at one o'clock at night and then Sasha was in his element

3

by arranging parties in the only Biergarten there was in this little village. All the musicians and many people of the audiences, from music students having arrived by bicycle from Finland, Denmark and Spain etc., to the rich ladies of Park Avenue, drank wine, listening to the nightingales and to the improvised music performances from Bach to Pop— Sasha always being in the center, telling stories or playing Viennese waltzes. Throughout all the years, following the last Casals Festival in France in 1953, I was in touch with Sasha from time to time. The telephone conversations usually started by him asking "Do you still sit on your "toches" (Jewish for "behind") making telephone calls?"

Yanna Kroyt Brandt:

It's hard to know where to begin to pay tribute to a man who knew me before I was born, who held me in his arms when I was a baby and who never quite accepted me when I finally grew up. My memories are so rich and varied. Most of all, I remember his warmth, his humor, his generosity, and his charm, mixed in with heavy doses of stubborness. He could also be surprisingly tactful and delicate. When I was in college, I visited him at his apartment on Beekman Place, overlooking the East River, where he lived with his girlfriend. He undoubtedly thought that I would be scandalized by his living arrangement and went to great lengths to protect me from the knowledge. He of course never suspected that I knew, and that at the age of 17, I found it wildly romantic.

He was there at many important events in my life, my wedding, for one, at which he played. His wedding gift was unusual and typical – a treasured set of three rare books of Delacroix drawings, a few prized pieces of antique silver. Since I knew what it meant for him to give them up, they were all the more treasured. Years later, he was also there for me and my family when my father died, staying with us, offering love and comfort at an immensely painful time. The myth that followed the Budapest Quartet was that they stayed together in public because they were never together in private. In fact, they were there for each other time and time again, in happy moments as well as tragic ones.

In the early days of Marlboro, where my family spent its summers, he was a fixture. He always insisted on finding unique places to live, and Marlboro was no exception. He bought an abandoned one–room schoolhouse, moved it to a wonderful plot of land and spent his summers there, doing what he probably loved best, making music with young people. He entertained often and joyously. He was always the life of the party, sometimes donning a wild, ridiculous blonde wig and dancing, singing, telling jokes. . . including some very naughty ones.

He was, of course, an extraordinary musician in many ways. When I was a teenager, I went to a concert of his at Dumbarton Oaks, in Washington. He had left the [Budapest] Quartet at that time and had gone on to be with Casals in Prades. When he came back, he gave a series of concerts of Bach suites for unaccompanied violin. He was crippled at the time, having circulation problems, in great pain, and unable to stand. But his time with Casals had seeped through his soul, and his playing was extraordinary, among the most moving performances of the Bach suites I have ever heard.

When he rejoined the Quartet, the other members relaxed; the prodigal son had returned and all would be all right once again. He had matured, his musicianship had deepened, and it enriched the Quartet.

In later years, we drifted apart and I saw him infrequently, at an occasional concert, at the health club where we were both members, on the occasion of Rudolf Serkin's memorial concert. I felt that I reminded him of the past and that came between us in a strange way. He was not a man to dwell on the past, he was far too immersed in the present.

Above all, he loved young people. He loved working with them, teaching them, inspiring them. And they loved him back. It was like being in touch with a moment in history, a tradition, a way of seeing and feeling, a robust love of life that seems rare today. Alex never did anything halfway. His heart and soul were committed to his every action. He never had children, much to his sorrow. So he lavished his attentions and his love on his niece, Natasha, with whom he shared a rare intimacy.

For me on Tuesday, February 2, when Abrasha died, my last link with my childhood in Europe died. I will always love him. I will always remember him. And although I saw him very infrequently in recent years, I will always think of him as family and I will always miss him.

David Sackson:

Shortly after I got out of the Army in 1945, I met Sasha, and we became very good friends – he referred to us as "The two most successful 2nd violinists in the business." I had been with the Gordon String Quartet, the leading quartet in America at that time. He arrived in the U. S. with the Budapest.

I remember vividly one hot summer day driving up to Connecticut with Sasha. He had a roadster – top down, singing away... we had bought Italian bread, sausage, two bottles of red wine, stopped along the way, pulled off the road at a picnic site and devoured the food and wine. We were heading for the house of one of Columbia Records' engineers to play in some experimental quartet recordings, working in the concept of quadraphonic sound. The quartet was Sasha and I, Karen Tuttle and George Ricci. We set up on a large lawn at the back of the house, each microphone, (one in front of each stand) some 30 feet from the other, with heavy electric wires leading into the recording machine in the house, some fifty feet away from the quartet. We didn't know exactly what was going on, but we were asked not to discuss with anyone what we had experienced. We were making recording history and didn't know it!

Thelma Lehmann:

Since 1947, when Sasha came to Seattle as a visiting professor for the School of Music at the University of Washington, he had periodically returned to play, to teach, or to visit good friends – almost always to live with us in our home.

Sasha's last visit was in February of 1992 when he came to fill the Lehmann Chair of Music at the University of Washington.

Sasha was a member of the world renowned Budapest String Quartet. Organizer of the Casals Prades and Puerto Rico festivals as well as the Marlboro and other glamorous music festivals. He was honored with the Kennedy Award in 1985. Isaac Stern is the only other violinist to earn this distinction.

Anyone familiar with the affairs of politics or music will know that wherever Sasha lands his restless nature would always leave an indelible mark.

It happened that in the summers of 1947 and 1948 he functioned as the visiting Walker Ames professor at the School of Music of the University of Washington. So in 1948 he acted as a catalyst in Seattle. Not only did his teaching have a great impact on almost all of the string members of the Orchestra, not only did he become a lifelong friend of

Eugene's and mine, but his deft hand masterminded what was often called the "1948 Revolution at the Seattle Symphony."

Whereas many other great musicians retired in their later ages, Sasha continued to enrich or revolutionize the music world with ever–fresh adventures.

Three great Russian violinists. Sasha with Ivan Galamian (center)violin teacher extraordinaire, and Joseph Gingold, famous concertmaster and teacher. Photo: T. Suárez.

Barbara Lilly:

I was one of a long line of Sasha's "Patricia Taylors." The name, and job, originated when he was playing with Ralph Kirkpatrick. He took the name "Patricia" from Kirkpatrick, and "Taylor" from the English for Schneider, and created a "Personal Representative" who typed his letters and arranged his concert dates. Thank goodness he took care of the airline and hotel reservations himself!

I got the job in 1949 through my friend Ellen Viner, the previous Patricia Taylor, who lived upstairs from Sasha at 31 Beekman Place. I was just back from Europe at the time and looking for work. Ellen had told me about Sasha's projects, but she hadn't described the man himself. Sasha was 41 at the time and darling — warm, funny, and overflowing with joie de vivre. It wasn't long before "Mr. Schneider" became "Sasha." He was such fun that when I got a full-time job, I kept working for him nights and weekends. I continued until September, 1955, when I married, left New York, and anointed Judy Schwartz as the next Patricia Taylor. I don't know about the other Patricia Taylors, but Ellen, Judy and I took dictation directly on the typewriter, smoothing out Sasha's English as we went along.

Once, backstage at Carnegie Hall, Sasha introduced me to two young women — previous Patricia Taylors — and took great delight in having the three of us meet. Patricia Taylor — his creation — had become an institution.

The phone rang one day while we were working and Sasha answered, then handed it over to me with a wicked grin. I should have guessed he was up to something, for none of my friends knew I was there. The call, for Miss Taylor, was from a woman in one of the out-of-town groups for which Sasha played. She was coming to New York and wanted to meet me over breakfast. I ended up making excuses at work and having breakfast at the Plaza. Sasha was delighted and amused. All I remember now about the morning is that there was a toaster plugged in at every table!

This February, I was at a meeting in New York when I saw a woman whose name tag read "Patricia Taylor." A real, honest-to-goodness, living, breathing Patricia Taylor! How I wished Sasha were still here so that I could have called and told him Patricia Taylor is alive and well and living at the Vista Hotel. I could imagine his laughter.

From time to time, over the years, I had gotten postcards or notes from Sasha, usually with the name Patricia Taylor

A faire aujourd'hui

in the return address. My copy of his autobiography is inscribed to Patricia Taylor. And the last note I have is from his "A faire aujourd'hui" pad, with a drawing of a couple coupling at the top. There'll never be another Sasha!

Carl Pruzan:

Sasha was a close friend, and I mourn his passing.

Whether or not you feel the enclosed undated letter from him is appropriate for public dissemination, its earthy language is so typical of Sasha, that his friends may savor it.

His letter is about Manuel Rosenthal, who many years ago was the conductor of the Seattle Symphony. Rosenthal and his "wife" were treated royally by the self–anointed cream of Seattle's society — who wouldn't think of inviting to dinner at their exclusive upright abodes, a married man and his illicit sex partner.

Rosenthal and his companion returned to Europe after the symphony season. When they tried to return to Seattle for the ensuing season, they were refused entry by the Immigration Service because Rosenthal had a real wife in Paris.

I am enclosing an "English translation" of Sasha's letter, with explanations in parentheses.

Saturday
Yes, I am ashamed of Seattle — the City in which I behaved so perfectly sexless during my two Summers! To give an example how to live the good old American Way, and after all this to read in the papers that a man – and a Frenchman foreigner, did come to live with a woman, sleep in the same bed with her, and the F.B.I. didn't have any idea that there was another one in Paris focking with somebody else!! — But anyway this will teach you Bastards a lesson that focking is permitted but not with your own wife, and don't call her your wife ever, Sonofa Beach. I still wont buy Oi, sters. Send now or never. (Referring to smoked oysters which he loved, originated in Seattle and which he discovered here, and which I occasionally sent to him.)
How do the Society Debutantes Lehmanns (Dr. Hans and Thelma Lehmann of Seattle, his and our close friends) feel about this focking business, and how is Eugene? Why doesn't he telephone sometimes? (Eugene Linden, former conductor here, now deceased.)
I am again a Batchelor of Arts, and focking just a la carte, and Semi–Annually

Yours,
S.

Gerhard Herz:

Sasha Schneider appeared with the Louisville Chamber Music Society over 40 times – that is more than any other artist in the (by now) 55 year old history of the Louisville Chamber Music Society. In addition to the ensembles, he performed the 6 solo Sonatas and Partitas by Bach (in 1950) and played duo recitals with Kirkpatrick, Istomin, Horszowski and Peter Serkin as well as trios with the Beaux Arts Trio and Piano Quartets with Luvisi, Trampler and Lesser. Before the Piano Quartet's last concert on September 20, 1980, Sasha received the honorary Doctor of Music degree from the University of Louisville on the basis of his 43 appearances in Louisville.

Among my memories, none is more vivid than an evening in 1956. Cellist Gregor Piatigorsky, in town to appear as soloist with the Louisville Orchestra, attended a concert by the Budapest Quartet and at intermission, went back stage to greet his old friends.

A great Russian embrace, with everyone shouting "Misha!" "Grisha!" "Sasha!" Kisses left, kisses right.

I turned to Sasha and said, " The Schubert C major!" (Schubert's Quintet in C major for two violins, viola and two cellos is one of the greatest works in the repertory, but seldom played because of its unusual instrumentation.)

The Budapest, as fate would have it, had played Schubert's quintet the night before in Indianapolis with a talented local cellist, and the music for it lay in the trunk of Sasha's car. A hasty conference was called, with Piatigorsky agreeing to play if he could perform the first cello part, since he had never played the second. A courier was dispatched to Piatigorsky's hotel to get his cello, while Fanny Brandeis, the Society's secretary, and Schneider went before the audience to announce "a lengthy intermission."

About an hour later, Piatigorsky joined The Budas on the stage of the University of Louisville Playhouse, (Schneider once remarked to me that the Playhouse had the second best acoustics in America and the dirtiest backstage facilities.)

I still remember the Schubert Quintet as one of the society's absolute high points, it was sheer heaven.

Raya Garbousova:

I mourn for Sasha. Our long friendship enriched me for many decades. They were full of agreements (and often disagreements).

One night about midnight the phone rang and what I heard was someone playing on the viola the cello prelude of the C major Bach suite. It was not difficult for me to guess who the long distance caller was, as Sasha was preparing a viola recital for the New School of Music, playing all six cello Bach suites. At the end, before I heard the player's voice, I shouted: "Sasha, why are you playing so fast?" I was right, it was Sasha, he shouted back: "I just had such stage fright, plus it costs too much playing it over the phone long distance at the proper tempos!"

Coming a few times for dinner to his house, I found with him a lovely woman friend. According to him he was attempting to live a peaceful life. When returning some time later, Sasha's friend was gone. The reason he gave me was that although she was really nice, life had become too monotonous.

Milton Katims:

Knowing and making music with Sasha, first with the Budapest and then even more closely in the New York Piano Quartet from 1939 to 1954, I knew and admired Sasha very much. He brought a zestful and alive love for music that was contagious. We didn't always agree but it was never dull! I have so many vivid memories of our friendship and music association that I'm not sure where to begin – these memories are flooding back into my mind now.

Ira Hirschman (New Friends of Music) engaged me to play the Mozart g minor Quintet with the Budapesters. I met with them in the Great Northern Hotel on West 57th. And even at that first musical meeting I was immediately aware of Sasha's being the electric spark of the quartet. Subsequently I had the joy of being part of this music making which was ever fresh – alive.

Jean–Pierre Rampal:

We were recording the Mozart flute quartets on a Christmas Day, – Isaac Stern, Sasha Schneider on viola, Leonard Rose on cello, and myself. After many hours of difficult work, we finally finished. Leonard and Isaac left to be with their families. Sasha said to me, "Come home with me, Jean–Pierre. This will be a special experience for you, to enjoy a wonderful Christmas dinner cooked by a Jew!"

Loren Glickman:

Sasha told me of his youthful days in Vilna. At the age of 14 or 15, he played nightly in the local whorehouse in a trio with brother Mischa and a pianist. (Remember this was before radios or recordings.) There was an upright piano in the sitting room. The trio played while the customers became acquainted with the ladies–of–the–night. There was also an upright piano in some of the fancier rooms upstairs, and on many occasions when a wealthy client wished to be serenaded while he took his pleasure, the trio would perform in the "room of pleasure," to the accompaniment of all the attendant sounds that one may imagine. At the end of the week, the trio received its pay. The following morning, Papa Schneider would confront young Alex, arm outstretched, and say "Give me your pay envelope." Sasha would hem and haw, shifting from one leg to another, and finally mumble "I spent it last night, Papa!" "What!" exclaimed Papa Schneider, "You spent it all on those whores again, after all I have said." And he accompanied this statement with a resounding slap in the face!

Apparently even at that early age, Sasha was very macho, for he told me this scene between father and son was repeated many, many times until he was finally forced to work elsewhere to help support the family.

Emmy Macauley Smith:

Who remembers Sasha's fantasy? The giant record of all the Haydn Quartets he would make to fill Columbus Circle – it would play round the clock. I never pass Columbus Circle without laughing.

I remember when Miecio Horszowski moved into an apartment up Riverside Drive – to "Keep house." Well we all went to work supplying him with the necessary items. I asked Sasha: "Does he have a double boiler?" Sasha answered: "He doesn't even have a Boiler!"

Together we wrote a cookbook. How to cook a minute steak: Put it on the fire and play the "Minute Waltz."

When Miecio was ill, Sasha prepared food and carried it to him – from 20th Street!

I find a Christmas card with loving words.

Sasha learned that there were fine wines across the river in Indiana; odd lots from Chicago that often included rare items at low prices. So we loaded up. "How will you get them home?" "Oh Gerhard (Herz) will bring them." "Lee will bring them." So of course they sat at the farm – "Where are my wines?" asked Sasha. So finally I packed 2 or 3 loads and sent our man Clifton to the Post Office (all very illegal). I did include home– made jelly.

"So what is this?" Clifton's answer might have been in Chinese, but intelligible was: "Jams and Jellies – Jellies and Jams." So Sasha finally got his wine.

Stan Gilson:

I first heard Sasha with the Budapest. Then, in the late 40's when I was a student at the University of Chicago, Sasha arrived to play a concert of Bach works for unaccompanied violin. It was midwinter, the coldest in history, and Chicago was in the throes of a coal strike... we all thought that Sasha would cancel the concert, but he did not.

Students and faculty, we all sat in the huge hall, stuffed into layers of sweaters and overcoats and wool caps. Our breath came steaming out of our mouths as though we were all smoking. At the center of the stage was a small electric heater. Sasha came out in an overcoat and cap and gloves and, of course, with his violin. And standing in front of that electric heater he took off the gloves and started to play. Oh how he played. The notes just flew.

It was magic.

Barbara Lilly:

Working with Sasha was full of the unexpected. One day he said to me: "Take a letter to the president of the Pennsylvania Railroad. 'Dear Sir: Today I took your train number xx from New York to Washington and bought a roast beef sandwich for $2.50. Enclosed is the roast beef sandwich.' " I have to say it was the poorest, most dried–up excuse for roast beef I'd ever seen. And $2.50 then was no small sum. Sasha was paying me $1.50 an hour.

Sasha had a delicious sense of humor. A woman I know tells of the time he told her "Every night I must make luff to a different woman." "Do you realize that's 365 women a year?" she answered. Sasha's reply — "Vye do you think I live in New York?"

Norman Carr:

I worked with Sasha for many years – primarily in the 50's and 60's. We performed in New York, (New School, Carnegie Hall etc.) Washington (Dumbarton Oaks) Puerto Rico, South and Central America, Mexico etc. Many recordings with Sasha and Casals. He was probably the single most important influence on my musical life. There were lots of good times and an incredible amount to remember. But what I will never forget is my initial experience with him.

In the late 40's I was introduced to Sasha by Danny Saidenberg and Mitch Miller. I was anxious to study Bach with him, especially after hearing him perform all the unaccompanied sonatas at 2 performances at the 92nd Street YMHA.

After my first two hour session, I asked what I owed him. He asked: "Where are you working?" "I'm not, at the moment" I replied – to which he answered "So how can you pay me? We'll talk about payment when you have a good job." He coached me for 6 months without any payment. In addition, he made sure I was in the chamber orchestra when he recorded the Mozart D Major.

There was nothing more important in Sasha's life than the making of music. An incredibly important part of my musical life died with Sasha – But God – what memories!

David Sackson:

Once I asked Sasha, "Why do you guys (Budapest Quartet) play so fast?" – He bellowed, "That son –of –a– bitch!" – I said "Who do you mean?" – He said: "That Toscanini – When we were still in Europe, before coming to America, we would hear Toscanini, whose tempi were very fast, so we thought that is the way it's done in America, so we played fast!"

Tina Rudie:

The first time I was with Sasha was in Perpignon, France, during the 1953 Casals Festival. There are many unforgettable impressions of him from that summer, but the best one involved getting to know him on the evening he gathered up a few of us to go to dinner on the spur of the moment. We followed his car down toward the Mediterranean, along over dirt roads through the marshes – finally stopping at a rough looking shack, a most uncommercial looking place sitting in the dark near the water. Entering the dusky place was a revelation. Sasha was greeted with such an overwhelming welcome! It was marvelous! Fishermen, laborers, cooks, waiters, were all so delighted to see him and smother him with bear hugs and kisses – tears of joy – much hoopla and hollering. I've never seen such a welcome. The dinner – fresh from the sea – was extraordinary and in keeping as I later learned, with Sasha's talent and appreciation of fine food. But the food not withstanding, the scene when we arrived was worth a trip from anywhere.

Loren Glickman:

Some time in the late thirties Sasha was engaged to play the six solo partitas and sonatas of Bach at Town Hall. The fee was to be $2000. Sasha communicated with Pablo Casals and said something on the following order: "Maitre Casals, I have always deeply admired your concepts of Bach. I have been engaged to perform the six solo violin works next fall, and if you are willing, I would like to study those works with you in the summer. My fee for performing is $2000, and I would like to offer you $2000 for the lessons." Casals agreed, Sasha went to France, and thus began the long friendship between the two artists.

Clara Reisenberg Rockmore:

Abrasha was one of my closest longtime friends. Whenever anything good or bad was happening to him, he would talk to me about it. He was like a leit–motif throughout my life.

I remember when he went to study the Bach solo sonatas with Casals. He told of his first lesson. Casals asked him to begin with the famous d–minor Chaconne. He began with the well–known chords, and Casals walked away and left the room, closing the door behind him. Abrasha was dumbfounded! Soon the door opened slowly and Casals entered tentatively, walking on tiptoe. "This is the way you played the opening," said Casals. "You should have played like this!" Whereupon he again walked out, and then opened the door very forcefully and strode through the entrance like a conquering hero! Sasha knew then how to play the opening chords.

Milton Katims:

When Sasha was performing the Six Bach Solo Sonatas and Partitas, he complained to Casals that the audience, with their many different editions of the score, turning pages at different times, was a terrible distraction while he was playing. Casals suggested that the solution was quite simple – close your eyes. At the very next concert in Sanders Hall at Harvard, Sasha was in the middle of the g minor fugue when he heard some discreet coughing behind him. He thought that it was strange – there had been no one on stage when he started – perhaps some people had quietly slipped in after he started. But Sasha was determined not to let it bother him – he continued to keep his eyes shut while he played – resulting in more and more coughing. He finally finished the fugue and opened his eyes. While playing he

19

had turned completely around. He was playing with his back to the audience and they were trying to bring it to his attention. (Casals didn't have that problem.)

Marjory Hanson:

It happened not too long after I stared to work for Sasha in the fall of 1956. The Budapest Quartet had been on a concert tour and were playing a concert on a college campus right after the Russians had taken over Hungary (Russian tanks sweeping Budapest, etc.). At the intermission the Quartet was sent a message by some students asking them to please play the Hungarian national anthem, in sympathy for what happened in Hungary. The members of the Quartet were nonplussed as to what to do. As Sasha said: "Ve are all Russians; ve Russians had taken over the Quartet."

Loren Glickman:

In the mid–fifties, we began playing concerts at the New School. Sasha programmed on three successive Sundays the 12 Concerti Grossi Op. 6 of Handel, scored for strings and harpsichord. The concerts were a huge success, and after the last, the audience kept insisting on another and another bow from Sasha and the other soloists. I stood offstage (not being a string player) applauding along with everyone else. Suddenly, as Sasha was about to lead the soloists on for yet another bow, he grabbed my hand and said "You come too!" "But Sasha," I protested, "the audience will not understand what I am doing out there." "It's all right," he replied, dragging me out to take a bow with him. "They'll think you are Handel!"

At one concert at the New School, Ralph Kirkpatrick was the harpsichord soloist. Sasha always took a great deal of time and effort with accompaniments, unlike other conductors who often barely brushed over accompaniments. On this occasion, working on the Bach d minor concerto, Sasha spent at least an hour before Kirkpatrick arrived, training the orchestra in how and where to play the accents, specifically in the first movement. Finally Ralph took his place at the keyboard. After a few minutes, Kirkpatrick, a very gentle man, got up and whispered something to Sasha, who then said, "A little less accent here."

The rehearsal continued. Kirkpatrick again stood up and whispered in Sasha's ear. Sasha said, "Listen, Ralph. We are friends. None of this conductor business. Say whatever you wish to the orchestra." Ralph said, "O.K., Sasha," and then proceeded to completely undo all the work that Sasha had so painstakingly done with the orchestra. Sasha looked like he was about to cry, but in a quiet voice, said to the orchestra, "Please do whatever Ralph asks you to do!"

Sasha was both unconventional and irrepressible. At another concert at the New School, Sasha and the orchestra had assembled on stage and were about to begin, when Sasha realized he had left his music–reading glasses in the tuning room a floor below. Not wishing to make the trek downstairs and the subsequent climb up to the stage, he stood up, shaded his eyes with his hand, and looking out to the audience, called out "Misha, are you out there?" "Ja, Sasha, I am here" answered Misha. "Do you have your reading glasses with you?" "Of course, Sasha. Here they are." Misha came to the stage, Sasha took the glasses, the audience was convulsed in laughter, and the concert was a grand success.

Sheila Bakerman Gilson:

For many years we have been going to the New School Concerts listening to Sasha and his friends play their beautiful music. We would always go downstairs to the green

21

room after the concerts to share the cheese and wine with the musicians. I would go over to Sasha and tell him how much I enjoyed the concert, and how it moved me in a very special way.

After one especially memorable performance I walked over to Sasha to tell him how dynamic his playing was and he said to me: "Are you an old girlfriend of mine?" and he gave me a hug. I said "no, – but yes, Sasha, I feel like an old girl friend... I'll never forget the joy you have given me all these years."

Marjory Hanson:

Sasha could be terribly generous and warmhearted. One day at the office, he was standing next to my desk and talking in an excited way. Somehow, he managed to knock over a glass of tomato juice I had on my desk. I watched with horror as the red fluid flowed all over some freshly typed documents. Sasha apologized profusely and later returned with a huge can of tomato juice and a fifth of vodka – so I could make lots of Bloody Marys! (No, we did not drink at the Festival Casals office; there was enough giddiness as it was!)

Herbert Sorkin:

One recollection of Sasha which comes to mind is of an evening at Marlboro, where I had been rehearsing some string quartets with a group which consisted, at various times, of Sasha himself, either coaching or playing 2nd violin; Arnold Steinhardt, who switched between 1st violin and viola with Michael Tree, Leslie Parnas on cello, and me, also switching, but usually between 2nd violin and viola. Subsequently that group (with the additions of John Dalley

22

and David Soyer, and subtractions of Sasha, Parnas and me) became the Guarneri Quartet.

We had been working on a Bartok quartet, it was late, we were all tired. Sasha suggested we call it a night, but someone, possibly both Steinhardt and Tree, asked Sasha to read a Haydn quartet before we quit for the night. Sasha agreed to read just one, after which he invited all of us to the room he rented in the house of a rather remarkable woman who may have been a librarian for Marlboro College. In any event, she was impressively literate and welcomed Sasha's extension of her hospitality.

Sasha, over bread, cheese, sausage and whatever good drink he happened to have there, allowed himself to be drawn into reminiscences of the Budapest Quartet. Had they played all the Haydn quartets? No, they didn't care to, just the famous ones. Had Sasha ever played all the Haydn quartets? Yes! Once. With a group of amateurs. They had gone to a retreat in the country, with some of their wives, and played day and night for about three days, stopping occasionally for a small repast or a few hours' sleep.

I do not remember all the details (it was about forty years ago). But the net impression, then and now, was of a very warm, vibrant camaraderie, all the more impressive because of Sasha's obvious respect for the younger people present.

Barbara Park Racusen:

Sasha changed my life.

Thirty years ago I had lost my only child, my mother and my husband – all within 18 months. I was a pain–filled wreck, withdrawing from friends and activities, even forsaking my sculpture. The Budapest String Quartet came to Burlington to perform and I was talked into giving a small reception in my home for them. That was the beginning of my long friendship with Sasha. It evolved into a rich variety of expanded interests and opportunities. Again, at Sasha's scolding, I worked in my sculpture studio. Occasionally I went to New York and Sasha invited me to his home for a great bouillabaise or he'd take me to shop at his favorite little stores for greens, fruit, breads, fresh coffee beans. His verve and enthusiasms were infectious whether music, art, politics or teaching.

David Soyer:

Some years ago, Sasha was giving a lecture on Haydn at the 92nd St. Y. When he was just about at the end of the lecture, he couldn't remember how he had intended to close. Finally in desperation, he said, "Do you know why Haydn lived such a long life? Because he didn't have syphilis!"

Barbara Lilly:

Sasha's enthusiasms were enormous and far–ranging. He fell for a Russian–style fur hat I'd bought in Canada, and insisted I get one for him, too. He brought back a lot of primitive paintings done by an elderly Israeli, long before they were news here. When I, in turn, said I had to have one, he got one for me, too. He displayed with delight things he'd picked up here and there — a set of soup bowls, a magnetic memo pad, an old ironstone platter, a book of drawings, a frying pan. I remember his trophies from a concert in New Orleans — a huge brass bed and a trunk full of Belle Watling era dresses, the contents of a nineteenth–century whorehouse that were being auctioned off. Who but Sasha would have bought things like that back then? His taste was unique — and unerring.

Modell av Vasa.
Finns i modellbyggsats.

Here is my way of enjoying how to Travel !! You ofcourse are Interested in Koppkess P.R. I had only two operations last week & have to stay put for another two weeks. If You need a fiddler or Conductor dont call me only visits are accepted, so Photo and I love to see You both.

all the best

Sasha

10044
Färgfoto: Johan Jonson
printed by giovanni trimboli   ⊗ ESSELTE

A postcard from Sasha: mid 1980's. Kopkess P.R. *refers to money to be made in Puerto Rico at the Casals Festival where Glickman and Schneider played for twenty years.*

25

Gordon and I moved to blue–law Pittsburgh in 1956, and one Sunday the phone rang. "Vere do you get a drink in this town?" said a familiar mellifluous voice. "Why, right here, Sasha," Gordon answered. We were giving a dinner party and Sasha and Mischa came over and made the party. Sasha would feed lines to Mischa who would bounce them back. It was a real brother act, and I'd never seen Mischa, the quieter one, so exuberant.

Sidonie K. Lederer:

In the many times I have seen Sasha Schneider, I never had the temerity of addressing him personally and yet had a sort of nodding acquaintance with him. Now that my memory is beginning to play tricks, recalling encounters with him is an impossibility.

Even as a teenager in an upstate city, I had heard of the Budapest Quartet. I think I found out at that time that Sasha and Misha were natives of Vitebsk, and since my mother was born in the ancient city of Polotsk, in that area, I felt like a sort of kinsman! I also retain a recollection of attending a concert with Sasha as the sole artist, playing intricate violin works – unaccompanied. On that long distant occasion he was an impressive performer.

When I went to Puerto Rico in 1956(?) for the first season of the Casals Festival, it was Sasha who took charge when Casals fell ill. He accomplished miracles by not only holding that diversified group together, but in giving us memorable music, even at rehearsals, aided and abetted by people like Walter Trampler, Loren Glickman, Sidney Harth, Julius Levine et al; all of this I recall with poignancy. All the subsequent years of attendance at that festival did not have such an impact, although every visit marked the highlight of the year for me.

The 23rd of April is celebrated as the day of Shakespeare's birth (and death, too). It seems a touching day for a tribute to one man, Sasha, who has contributed so extensively, so nobly, and so effectively to the nurture of the holde Kunst in our country.

Greg Schneider:

This is the Sasha I knew. He was my Uncle Brasha, as a child, who carried an instrument and had many people rave about his " wine, women, and song," but more than that he was my romantic cowboy. He had a "white horse," which he drove all over the country and I was led to believe, world. When Uncle Brasha came to visit us he always had gifts and a drawl that the cowboys of Texas and Oklahoma would have. He would then get on his knees and hands so we could have a ride on his back. In the late 50's, Uncle Brasha got rid of his "white horse" by driving it off some cliff. Only a real cowboy would get rid of his prized horse in such a manner. After the "white horse" left the scene Uncle 'Brasha gradually became known as Uncle Abrasha. I came to respect him for his professional music and gourmet. However, I remember a warmth and appreciation for me and my brother, Mark. He gave of his time, appreciation for life and often gave us the encouragement and support that only an uncle could, who roamed the earth as a cowboy.

Uncle Abrasha, I love and respect you. You will always be in my memory.

Thanks for what you provided to music and gourmet, but thanks most of all for not forgetting the importance of family.

Rene A. Morel:

To tell you all of which I had experienced with Sasha would be too long. But I can never forget the way I met him. It was sometime during the year of 1956.

I was then working in the shop of R. Wurlitzer under Maestro Sacconi. Sasha had left his two bows for rehair the day before. The next day when most of the employees were out to lunch, and being in the shop by myself, Sasha came down a narrow staircase leading to the shop. When he was still four or five stairs up he started yelling "are my bows ready?"

My English was very poor, but I knew enough to say "Yes, Sir!" Right away in French he said to me "Tu es Francais? Merde alors qu'est ce que tu fais ici? Where are my bows?" This was my first introduction to Sasha. Still on his fourth step I brought him the two bows. He took a look at them and said "That is a lousy job. This is the old hairs that you washed with alcohol, and don't tell me no! I did this before you, when I was young." Feeling very intimidated, I was afraid to answer, but I assured him that this firm was honest and we did not do such things. He remained very serious and continued saying, "I will not come back here, because etc., etc." I became somewhat annoyed. I took my courage into my hands and with a raised sounding voice, and in French of course, I respectfully gave him a piece of my mind. He listened carefully, and with a big laugh he said "I like you. You will go far, and I am sorry if I offended you". From that time on we became good friends.

Ann Neubauer:

My memories of Sasha go back to Marlboro, Vermont, in the 1950's and 60's, to the Casals Festival in Puerto Rico, the many, many New School concerts including Sasha's 60th

28

birthday celebration, Christmas concerts at Carnegie Hall including midnight performances, and Le Paradou, Sasha's country home in Provence.

How and why did we get to Le Paradou? It was at a New York concert that Sasha asked my husband, Ernest Neubauer, whether we would be coming to Europe again on our summer vacation. If so, would Ernest please stop at Le Paradou to take care of the grand piano which badly needed attention, and there was no one there who could do it the way he did, and had done for some twenty years in Sasha's New York City home. Although Sasha would not be there, we were invited to stay at his home which was looked after by a caretaker who would welcome us.

And so we went to Le Paradou ("Paradise"), driving from Switzerland following Sasha's travel directions, to the little village consisting of one "main" street where English was not spoken and French was hard to understand because of the local Southern accent. However – we managed. While Ernest worked on the piano, I shopped in the local markets, sometimes forgetting to take along a basket for my purchases as is the custom, plastic or paper bags being unknown – and how do you carry half a dozen eggs home with you if you forget — like I did?!

Sasha's home, a farmhouse equipped with modern conveniences – but no air conditioning (and it was hot, in mid–July!) was comfortable and spacious. We explored the beautiful countryside; Paradou is located between Arles and Avignon, a most fascinating region. Ernest put the piano into top shape, which resulted in our being asked again the following summer!

Sadly, Sasha is no longer with us, and neither is Ernest, but of course, the memories of those summer weeks at Le Paradou, and the many, many hours of music making that Sasha gave to all his friends will remain forever.

Marjory Hanson:

One year, when I happened to be working in the Festival Casals office on my birthday – and Sasha had discovered it was my birthday – he left the office for awhile. Suddenly, the door to the office opened and in came Sasha and Felix Galimir, both with their violins tucked under their chins, and playing "Happy Birthday to You!" He also gave me, as a birthday present, a copy of the book Lolita, which was all the rage at the time and somewhat of a scandal.

Loren Glickman:

When I first began to contract orchestras for Sasha's concerts – it was a good while before we became warm friends – we were playing a concert in Carnegie Hall at midnight on Christmas Eve. The orchestra played a short symphony first, then left the stage, and Sasha came on to play the Bach d minor partita for solo violin. Standing offstage in the wings, I was in awe of his artistry, and of the awesome situation of standing on the Carnegie Hall stage, before a packed house of some 3,000 people, and performing this most difficult work almost flawlessly for some 40 minutes. When he finished the great Chaconne to end the work, the audience gave him a wild standing ovation. As he walked toward the wings, I, like a child, waited breathlessly to hear what important words this great artist would have to say. He passed out of the audience's line of sight, looked at me, and said – – – "Oy, my feet hurt!"

A little fun time. Photo: T. Suárez.

Carol Wincenc:

The news of Sasha's passing was so saddening indeed. He has a special place in my past and he gave so much to me both musically and personally. Here is one of my most favorite recollections:

It is a typically snowy evening in Buffalo, New York – sometime between 1956–58 and my family and I (at grammar

31

school age) are off to Baird Hall to hear the Budapest Quartet. The concert hall is packed with people – an overflow crowd and stage seats are necessary. The happy and intense anticipation of yet another memorable evening of consummate quartet playing awaits us all. Suddenly my mother rushes me onstage to one of the front row stage seats. There I was, with pigtails and wide eyes beholding the group. Suddenly my eyes meet with Sasha's. His face is so animated and alive with emotion and concentration but to my shock he is managing to wink at me and even flirt while negotiating tricky passage work!! How can this be??!! I continue in this exchange with him with both disbelief and pure enchantment. What a charmer this man was!

Needless to say, I couldn't contain my amazement after the concert – and this began a relationship with this dynamic individual.

To my thrill, I was able to make music with Sasha some 30 years later and the charm and sincerity never skipped a beat. I so loved this man and what he gave and how he shared his long, virile light with so many.

Loren Glickman:

In the mid–fifties, we were engaged to perform and record "L'Histoire du Soldat," the Octet, and the new Septet, under the baton of the composer, Igor Stravinsky. At the first reading rehearsal, all was going very well until we got to the Tango movement, which is mainly a violin solo, accompanied by percussion. Sasha played – Yum.... taTa, ta .. tatatataTum. Stravinsky stopped, incredulous, and said, "Sasha, I did not write Yum .... taTa, ta.. tatatataTum! I wrote Yum .. ta . Ta, ta . ta–ta–ta–ta Tum!" Sasha replied "Igor," (or whatever was the Russian dimunitive he used), "didn't you ever dance a tango in Paris?" And with that, he stood up and began dancing the tango around the room. "I *must* play Yum .... taTa, and not Yum . . ta. Ta!" Confronted with such a display of "tango–verve," Stravinsky sheepishly agreed that Sasha's tango was much more in "style" than his own dry version, and following the release of our recording, Sasha's rendition became the accepted way to play Stravinsky's tango!

William Sallar:

I knew you as a violinist
In a famed quartet
Decades ago,
And in later chamber music
For your gifts of Haydn.
As violinist and conductor
And creating orchestras for youth,
And at eighty
       still conducting,
       still delighting:
You are Prospero of the
       isle of music
You've been ruling so
       benignly,
And so long.

Barbara Lilly:

When I began working for Sasha, he was living on Beekman Place and it was the Margaret Bourke White era. That relationship ended, and Sasha would often go off about ten at night to a Turkish bath and dinner in Chinatown with Gjon Mili. They were great friends, and Sasha must have felt a tremendous sense of loss when Mili died. I remember

First Time in the U.S.A.
After a trans-continental tour which lasted 50 years and shattered the world

The Greatest Violinist
Original
Schmoekedores
only 50 more years available

PROGRAM
1. Scales
2. More Scales
Intermission
3. Kreutzer Etude #2
   with all variations
Encores

at the Steinway
another
Schmoekedores

October 21, 1958   10:30 P.M.
GJON MILO'S BISTRO   6 East 23rd Street
Doors will be closed at 5 A.M.

Sasha's 50th birthday party at Gjon Mili's

34

the fiftieth birthday party Mili gave for Sasha in his studio. Guests came from all over — we ran into each other again that night at the airport — and Mili organized a marvelous show.

Sasha had to leave the Beekman Place apartment when the building was sold (some said to the sister of the Shah of Iran) and he found a large floor–through at 21 East 11th St. By then he had met Geraldine Page and he was absolutely besotted by her. I remember the preparations for their honeymoon in Europe — Gerry's first trip abroad. Sasha laid out on the bed all the clothes she had bought under his worldly guidance (or maybe he had bought them without her) and Gerry was as thrilled as if she were a girl from the sticks. I also remember the breakup in 1955. I was very upset.

One night, in Pittsburgh, we met Sasha for a drink after a concert and were joined by a pretty blonde college student. Sasha had been making eyes at her in the balcony while he played. — And never missed a beat!

Keith Brown:

My wife and I were invited to a party at Gjon Mili's studio on 23rd Street, the evening of October 21, 1958. The invitation that was sent had a photo of Sasha in a bandsman's coat playing a small fiddle – with the usual reference, "The Greatest Violinist Original Schmoekedores."

I was told that Casals would be there – he was, and very much the guest of honor. I remember Sardanas, Bach (particularly the second Brandenburg), etc. It was a wonderful tribute to Don Pablo. As we were leaving, I thanked Sasha for the best birthday party ever given me. His response, along with a sweaty bear–hug, was, "Your birthday? My birthday! WE' RE BROTHERS!"

He never forgot – through many festivals in Puerto Rico, l'Histoires in NYC, etc. – charging into shops at the Caribe

Hilton and the old town with comments such as, "Take good care of him; he's my brother." This always got an interesting (usually incredulous) response from the sales people.

That birthday with Sasha was his fiftieth (my twenty-fifth), and I remember with much love, his sixtieth, seventieth and others at the New School and at his loft on 20th Street – always special events – as was virtually everything that Sasha did. I owe him much. He was a special friend, a great musician – and I treasure my many years of music–making with him.

Al Howard:

Thanks Loren for sending the L'Histoire tape. Looking at it, – with Sasha, Stravinsky, and all the rest of the players, – meant a great deal to both Alice and myself.

My stories about Sasha are not too prolific, but there were some cherished moments:

When Sasha married Gerry Page, I gave them a wedding gift that Sasha just flipped over – I found an OLD bass drum that I had converted into a coffee table. On the bass drum was the lettering: 243rd ENGINEERS BATTALION. It was in big red letters and it ran around the entire edge of the drum. Sasha loved it! I wonder what happened to it after he and Gerry broke up.

Of course, Chinese food was a great love of Sasha's. Once we all went down to Wo Kee in Chinatown and Sasha got us a table in the kitchen so as to be nearer the preparation of his favorite food.

Another time after a performance of L'Histoire Du Soldat in Alice Tully Hall, I hired a double decker bus and we all went to Sasha's place on 23rd street for a mammoth party. Was that the time Danny Kaye and Casals came?

Sasha was a fanatical New York Giants baseball fan. I

was just as crazy over the Brooklyn Dodgers and we would have fierce (but loving) fights.

Sasha's favorite comment about Alice was : "Shayna Maydela." Alice just adored Sasha.

Karen Tuttle:

Next to Casals, I learned more from Sasha than from any other musical influence in my life.

Marjory Hanson:

This is my funniest story – involving amateur violinist Albert Einstein, who occasionally played chamber music with the Budapest Quartet.

I was at Marlboro and was present during a conversation between Sasha and Frank Salomon or it may have been Tony Checchia.

Frank (or Tony): Sasha, I'd like to ask you about a story I heard involving Einstein and the Budapest.

Sasha: Shoot!

F (or T): Einstein was sitting in with the Quartet one day. Someone in the hallway overheard you shouting: " Vun, two, Vun, two! Dr. Einstein, ven vill you learn to count?!"

Sasha: (with a perfectly straight face) "Yeah, dot's true, Albert never did learn to count!"

Loren Glickman:

The Budapest Quartet used to play a regular series of concerts at the Library of Congress in Washington as the resident quartet. The magnificent Strad that had been Fritz Kreisler's and had been willed to the Library after Kreisler's

An almost oriental quartet. Sasha with Hiroko Yajima, vn; Nobuko Imai, vla; Ko Iwasaki, cello. Photo: Nobuko Imai

death, was kept on display in a glass case with the attendant history of its former owners. Whenever Sasha would come to the Library, he would get a guard to bring him the violin so that he could play on it for an hour or two. Subsequently, he began using the Kreisler fiddle during his concerts, while his own Strad reposed in the Library's display case. On a sudden impulse, one day he decided that the Kreisler Strad was too great an instrument to be wasting away in the glass case, so he left his own Strad with the unsuspecting guard, and played the Kreisler Strad a whole season, all over the world. On the day of the last concert at the Library that season, the guard brought Sasha his own violin, and Sasha returned the more famous Strad, and no one was ever the wiser.

One of Sasha's old friends was Abe Fortas, famous Washington lawyer and subsequently Justice of the Supreme Court. Fortas was also an amateur violinist (or violist), and on many occasions when in Washington, Sasha would bring some of his colleagues to play quartets with his good friend.

38

There came a terrible set of circumstances, when Richard Nixon who hated Fortas, dug up some disagreeable experiences in Fortas' past causing the Justice to resign, amid much unpleasant publicity. Sasha called Fortas to say he was coming to Washington with colleagues to play quartets that evening. Fortas said "Sasha! Of all days! Don't you read the papers? I'm being crucified!" Sasha replied, "Of course I read the papers, Abe. That's exactly the reason we will play quartets tonight!" And play they did.

Isidore Cohen:

Sasha used his personal linguistic invention, Schmoekadores, in many different ways to mean a variety of things. He might say "Play this passage with a little more Schmoekadores," meaning a little more emotion. Or, "Let's stop the Schmoekadores and get back to work." Or, "The greatest pleasures in life are making music, making chicken soup, and making Schmoekadores!"

Marjory Hanson:

One day at the Festival Casals office Sasha had me put through a call to an executive at G. Schirmer's. He wanted to discuss getting some music for an upcoming festival. His phone had different lines with buttons to push; he tended to be impatient and push any button that suited him. I told him that I had Mr. — of G. Schirmer's on line two. At the same moment, a call came through on line one from Dave Walter, bassist in that year's Festival Orchestra. Sasha pushed line one and began talking to Dave, thinking it was Mr. —— . Rather than enlightening Sasha, Dave answered his questions as though he was Mr. ——. But he gave increasingly ridiculous answers until an incredulous Sasha finally said,

"Is this Mr. — from G. Schirmer's ?" Dave replied; "No, this is Dave Walter from Brooklyn!" I then got on the phone with Dave while Sasha finally spoke to the caller from G. Schirmer's . I wish I could remember what Dave had said to Sasha. When I relayed the conversation to Dinorah Press, we both laughed until we had tears in our eyes.

Milton Katims:

When John Hammond (Mercury Records) brought Sasha, Mieccio Horszowski, Frank Miller and me together to form the New York Piano Quartet and record for Mercury, I began to have an even closer relationship with Sasha. I don't think you can find four more disparate musical personalities – but we admired and respected one another and the music making was always exciting. Much of the time Sasha and Frank were at each other's throats (figuratively, only once literally) – I was usually in the middle trying to calm them down – and, if things heated up too much, Mieccio left the room. Our rehearsals usually took place in Sasha's Beekman Pl. basement apartment, followed by beer, cheese and crackers. At one time we invited Phil Sklar, NBC Symphony solo bass, to join us for performances of the Schubert "Trout" Quintet. Phil and I lived out on Long Island. After one rehearsal, as we were driving home, Phil started to talk about Sasha and his very Bohemian life–style. Phil asked me if I thought Sasha was happy. I suggested that he ask Sasha at the next rehearsal. Four days later Sasha phoned me and said – "That son–of–a–beach Sklar asked me if I'm happy. I haven't slept three nights asking myself if I'm happy!"

Loren Glickman:

Sasha and I spent many hours each year discussing (arguing) over who would best fill each chair of the orchestra of the Festival Casals in Puerto Rico. Despite the often bitter arguments, we both knew the intention on both of our parts was to create each year the very best symphony orchestra which would also be receptive to Pablo Casals' artistic wishes.

On one occasion – I should at this point set the picture in his apartment: we sat across the table from each other, drinking wine, with a pile of papers before us, John Barrows, the great horn player, sat off in a corner reading a magazine – I brought up the name of Jerry Tarack. Jerry, a few years later became well known as a fine soloist and the concertmaster of many of New York's finer free–lance orchestras, but at the time he was not yet recognized, and Sasha was not yet aware of his abilities.

Sasha: "Tarack? No!"

L.G.: "Why not. You don't even know his playing."

Sasha: "Never mind. I know better."

L.G.: "That's not an answer. He's really a wonderful player."

Sasha: "No!, No!, No!"

L.G.: "I refuse to accept that! You must give a reason!"

Sasha: "All right! He sits like a statue and doesn't move with the music!"

L.G.: "That is a poor reason. He plays with warmth and artistry."

Sasha: "No! No! No! No! No!"

At this point, John Barrows came over and said, "Sasha, he really is a fine violinist. The reason he sits so still is because his eyes are very bad, and if he moves around, he loses focus on the music!" Sasha said "Ja? Well why didn't you say so in the first place? Of course we will take him in." Hours later, when John and I left the apartment, I said to him "Where did you get that horse–manure about Jerry's eyes?" John smiled and said, "I thought it would be a good way of ending that nasty argument!"

The above anecdote brings to mind three other occasions when Sasha and I were discussing(?) personnel. In the first, as our conversation turned argumentative, voices rising, imprecations being thrown at each other — louder and louder— suddenly in the midst of such clamor, Sasha exclaimed, with great passion "What do you want from me? So I *can't* play in tune!" I was so shocked by the sudden turn in his thinking to the personal, that I could say nothing. I put on my coat. Sasha and I embraced wordlessly, and I left. We never again referred to this incident.

One must remember that over a period of almost twenty years, Sasha and I spent many hours together, always late at night, shaping and reshaping the orchestra, trying to make it ever better than the year before. Our meetings were not always acrimonious, but frequently emotional. So, the second recollection finds us in the same situation as the one above (but probably years apart), arguing vehemently, voices louder and louder. Sasha begins to cry, and so do I, but the arguing continues. Suddenly, Sasha breaks off in the middle of a (screaming) reply, and shouts "Look at you! Your glass is empty! Why didn't you say so?" He then proceeds to fill my glass with whatever wonderful wine we were drinking, and then, as if there had been no interruption, continues the previous conversation with straining vocal chords, "You don't know nothing about music or musicians!"

The third of these recollections has nothing to do with temper (or intemperate remarks). It was midwinter, snow on the ground, cold wind blowing. Sasha and I meeting again in his apartment, the time is after midnight, more likely 2am. Throughout our meeting, Sasha would interrupt with, "You must try this wonderful Scotch I found. Here take home a bottle." And later, "Do you like this red wine? It's wonderful. Take a bottle." And "I just got a case of the smoothest white

42

Sample Repertoire as Violinist:

Scales
More Scales
INTERMISSION
Kreutzer Etude #2 with all variations
Encores

Sample Repertoire as Conductor:

Mahler—Symphony of a Thousand
Bruckner—Symphony #8 in c minor
INTERMISSION
Wagner—The Ring

Press Quotes:

"What style, what flair, a saint as soloist, his conducting Friday was as stimulating as ever. A legendary figure in international music circles, he has two trademarks, the violin and vitality." —THE ARIZONA REPUBLIC, MARCH 19, 1977

"Alexander Schneider, Dean of Chamber Music, adds touch of warmth. His enthusiasm and special radiance embrace audience and performers alike." —KANSAS CITY STAR, SEPTEMBER 30, 1979

"What stands out in a Schneider performance is the personality he imparts to every line. He could conduct the Montgomery telephone book and make a work of art out of it." —BIRMINGHAM NEWS, JANUARY 17, 1980

OCTOBER 21, 1980, 6P.M.
THE DAY HE WILL RECEIVE THE PERMANENT GRAND
EVERY MONTH FROM THE SOCIAL SECURITY
5 EAST 20TH STREET
DOORS WILL BE CLOSED AT MIDNIGHT

Sasha's Social Security checks begin.

43

wine. Take a bottle." So, after a few hours, besides planning the orchestra, Sasha had now prepared about ten bottles for me to take. I put on my overcoat, took my briefcase and my bassoon, and managed to carry about three bottles in addition. Sasha said, "I'll take the others down to your car" (which was parked in front of his building). I said, "Put a coat on. It's cold outside." But he waved off the suggestion, and went out in his shirtsleeves. As we were putting the various items into my car, very silently a police car had rolled up, and a very large policeman said, "Awright! Where do you guys think you're going wid that stuff?" I said, "This is Mr. Schneider. He lives here, and he has given me these bottles as a gift." Policeman: "Of course he has! But first, you took them from this store, didn't you?" LG: "Of course not! This store is a hardware store! And please let Mr. Schneider go inside. He'll catch pneumonia!" Cop: "Buddy, *I'll* tell *you* when he can go inside!" LG: "Look, officer, Mr. Schneider is a very famous man, and very generous. He lives upstairs. You can see the lights in his apartment. Please let him go inside before he really gets sick." The policeman mulls over the whole situation, and finally says, "O.K., it just looked suspicious. I guess you guys are all right. But my job is to protect the people who live here." I thanked him profusely, and as he drove off, I turned to the shivering Sasha and said, "Sasha! For God's sake, why didn't you say something? You never said one word!" And Sasha replied, "Vit my eccent, dey vould have sent me back to Russia!"

Marjory Hanson:

Sasha could be irascible. When I worked for him, he was still playing with the Budapest Quartet and they were on the road a lot. When he returned to the Festival Office, Nora Press and I were inundated with work. Sasha demanded our complete attention!

On one particularly hectic day, I had managed to slip out for a quick lunch, but Nora had been working without a break until mid–afternoon, at which time she said: "Sasha , I'm going down to get a cup of coffee and I'll bring it back up." Sasha blew up at both of us and said: "Vy can't you girls take your holidays ven I'm avay ?!?"

Paul Wolfe:

The time: Christmas week 1959; the place: Columbia Records, 30th Street, New York City; the record: Viennese Waltzes.

Sasha, with Willy Boskowsky, was probably the greatest interpreter of Viennese Waltzes in the world, so it was with much anticipation that I looked forward to two all night sessions with Walter Trampler, Felix Galimir and Julius Levine.

What a great experience! Sasha took fantastic liberties with these charming pieces, Felix followed him perfectly, Julius gave the down beats and Walter and I were, for the most part, the oompahs.

Then there came one waltz that called for only two violins and Sasha gave me one of the most difficult assignments I have ever had in my life: "Paul, go into the control booth and tell me when it is out of tune!"

That was an experience I'll never forget.

Claude Frank:

What can one say about Sasha with words that would be enough??? He has done so much, meant so much, inspired so much. Nothing is enough!!

Rehearsals with him were HIS, and there were no two ways about it. He ran them. Verbal contributions were automatically interrupted, or not listened to, or both. Only once, when I thought that something musical was important and HAD to be mentioned, I had to find a way of smuggling it in, and the only Possible way was this: "I saw Deep Throat last night!" "Wfffot??" With that he put his fiddle down, listened to the description of the x–rated movie, until I hastily put in: "And at letter B we are too slow!"

Very recently, we walked up Madison Avenue and talked about Horowitz. Now, Sasha was of course German– Viennese oriented about pianists. Schnabel was his old idol, and Serkin was his contemporary idol. Nevertheless Horowitz had an important place in his admiration. And his immortal appraisal of Horowitz, most emphatically expressed as was everything, was "Horowitz was the ONLY PIANIST who played in TOON!!!"

Sasha with Claude Frank, famous pianist. December 22, 1992. Reception at Carnegie Hall. "Re-mem-ber That Learn That (on shirt) Photo: Elizabeth Power.

46

Samuel Rhodes:

I have been fortunate enough to have had many contacts with Sasha, most of thm as a young musician before I joined the Juilliard String Quartet. I played with him both in his orchestra and in chamber music groups at the New School, Carnegie Hall, Washington Irving High School, the Festival Casals and Marlboro. Indeed, my first performance ever at Marlboro was with him, the Brahms Piano Quintet in 1960, and that was the first of many direct experiences of his intensely vital, fiery, totally committed music–making. He was not easy on me! His brutally frank comments on my shortcomings, though hard to bear at the time, were a major element in helping me to improve my skills and my artistry.

One of the most vivid memories I have is of a telephone conversation with him just after my father passed away. He had called me to invite me to a play in a concert he was planning. When he heard how distraught I was at the moment, he shouted roughly, "Work! Keep working intensely and that is how you will heal." I hear that voice within me today. It is one of those voices that echo inside my brain and helps to sustain me when I falter.

Milton Katims:

Sasha was always quite generous – with his time, his talent and with his money. I was just recalling his house in Roussilon (France) and our being invited, along with another couple, to use the house for a week or 10 days. Sasha recommended the cafe in town for our meals and when we attempted to pay for our meals, the proprietor informed us that Sasha had paid for all of our meals.

47

During all the years we were together I had already developed the bad habit of telling jokes when we paused for a rest. Sasha was a great audience (of course, he liked my stories) but he had difficulty remembering them. So he bought a little black book in order to put them down in writing. Many times, when I heard him retelling one of my stories, he inadvertently mangled it just enough to make it even funnier.

Sasha was one of a kind and I feel fortunate to have had a close relationship with him for over 50 years – through the Budapest years – the New York Piano Quartet – and the Casals Festivals. He added much to our lives!

Marjory Hanson:

Once at Kennedy Airport, before leaving for Puerto Rico, Sasha put his Guarnerius down for a minute and it mysteriously ended up traveling in the baggage hold of the plane. (We had made arrangements with Pan Am to have all the instruments in the cabin – including the string basses!). Sasha was displeased to say the least, but the Guarnerius survived!

Yosl Bergner:

One afternoon about 1961, a man with a sparkle in his eye – a man I had never met before – opened the door and came in and began a conversation with me. His language was very familiar to me. It was Anglo–Yiddish, Russo–Yiddish and Yiddish–Yiddish – in other words the ancient language of the lost Schmoekedores Tribe. Since I also belong to this tribe, we understood each other immediately and it became a lasting friendship between Sasha and me and my wife Audrey. It was music, drinking, quarreling, music, drinking, loving, music, drinking, music – and more drinking.

Suddenly Sasha fell in love – Russian love, suffering. He used to arrive, after hours of flying, from every corner of the world, just for a few days – but the beautiful lady was busy. So he suffered and loved. I advised the beautiful lady never to let him know that she loved him, because without suffering he was unable to love. Once there was a concert in Jerusalem to celebrate Israel's Independence Day. Sasha was conducting, and Arthur Rubinstein was playing. The atmosphere was festive and very exciting. The beautiful lady was so moved that after the concert she told Sasha that she loved him. Now, that was too much for the Russian soul of Sasha. He got drunk and came running to us in Tel Aviv in the middle of the night in a passion of tears. "Now? Now she loves me? And all that time I suffered?!"

But all that aside – the minute he began playing, conducting, teaching, Sasha's face changed and he became tense and serious. There was no more Schmoekedores. Sasha organized and inspired the first Israeli Music Festival in 1961, with Isaac Stern. It was Sasha who brought the Festival to the Roman amphitheatres in Caesarea and Beit Sha'an.

And beneath his great vivaciousness there was always the shadow of the narrow streets of Vilna. He didn't have to search for roots – he carried them with him wherever he went.

Lynn Harrell:

I was sixteen years old when I first met Mr. Schneider. It was Puerto Rico, the Casals Festival. He was on the podium to rehearse the orchestra: exhorting, shouting, crying out, angry and frustrated, always beseeching – with a passion and an energy that was searing. I had never come across

49

such naked, unkempt feeling in my life so far. I was both mesmerized and embarrassed, but in my consternation, he taught me one valuable lesson – that it was all for the music.

Thirty years later, he came to work with the students of the Los Angeles Philharmonic Institute and I saw on their faces the same bewilderment and inspiration. I felt part of the magic circle of his life and love for music.

Jinny and Paul Reinhardt:

We have known Sasha since his days at Mills College with the Budapest Quartet.

I was a Mills student and my husband Paul was the son of President Aurelia Reinhardt who is mentioned in Sasha's book, Sasha, A Musician's Life. When Sasha came to San Francisco (in recent years for the Mostly Mozart series) we always saw him afterwards, often for dinner.

June Schneider, Mischa and Sasha always called us when they came West. In those days at Mills, Mischa and Sasha were generous in playing cello and violin informally for their friends in Orchard Meadow Hall where I lived. When the Quartet had to drive to Chicago for a concert, I drove Mischa and his daughter Natasha, and other Mills girls drove Sasha.

We will greatly miss our warm visits with Sasha. We will miss his violin and his conducting. We will miss his great joi de vivre, his mischievous twinkle, his love and encouragement to young people, his superb talent, his generous sharing.

Arlene Gould:

I was fortunate to have gone to SUNY Buffalo from 1962 to 1966, during the final years of the Budapest String Quartet performances there. The quartet was in residence at the

Seminar, 1977. Photo: Tina Pelikan

University and each year they presented the Beethoven String Quartet cycle. At first I went because it was the thing for a budding intellectual to do, but very quickly I got hooked. My roommate and I used to speculate what each of the players was like offstage. Martha was convinced that the dynamic second violinist, who was in such great shape and moved so well, had a hot date after each concert. One time we actually saw him tear out the hall and, by golly, roar off in a red convertible with a sexy looking woman. By the time I was a senior, I had become an usher at all their concerts. Eventually I even worked back stage where it was my great thrill to hold the door for the quartet members as they went on and off stage. For me it was like meeting the gods on Olympus.

Tony Scelba:

Thanks for the invitation to the Schneider Memorial. Unfortunately, I'm working on the 23rd.

Long before the Casals connection, I met Schneider in 1967 in L.A. He was quite a fellow. At his concert, play an especially sweet note to Sasha for me.

Loren Glickman:

When Glenn Gould first came to the attention of Columbia Records, as a very young man, Sasha was asked if he wouldn't mind listening to Gould on the Budapest Quartet's next appearance in Toronto and giving Columbia his opinion. Sasha said he would be happy to do so, and when next in Toronto, called Glenn Gould and asked if he would play sonatas with him "the next morning". Gould said he would love to. "Which sonatas?" Sasha: "It doesn't matter. Whatever you wish." Gould: "But, specifically, which sonatas?" Sasha: "O.K. Mozart Bb major. Handel D major. Beethoven G major." The following morning, Gould showed up promptly at the appointed hour. They went to the hotel ballroom. Sasha tuned his violin, put his music on a stand, and only then realized that Glenn Gould did not bring any music. He had memorized the three sonatas agreed upon. As Sasha recounted the story: "There I was, having played these sonatas for 40 years with the music on my stand, and this young Schmoekedores memorized the sonatas overnight, and played them with great artistry! Naturally I recommended him to Columbia."

Sushu demonstrating how not *to "sqveeze de bow." (Don't hold it)*
Photo: Dorothea v. Haeften

Ansie Baird:

The Budapest String Quartet played at our wedding. Well actually it wasn't the Budapest String Quartet, because Joe Roisman wouldn't play that afternoon when they were performing a concert at Baird Hall at the University of Buffalo that very evening (Saturday Oct. 28, 1961), part of the annual Beethoven cycle which the Budapest played every year from 1955 on at U. B. So Sasha, Mischa and Boris Kroyt played the slow movement of a Beethoven trio at Trinity Episcopal Church before the ceremony marrying Brent Baird (son of their great friend Cameron Baird, who died in 1960) and Ansie Silverman (daughter of their great friend Oscar Silverman, who gave the bride away).

We all knew Sasha all our lives and it's hard to believe we will not hear that outrageous, joking, tender voice ever again.

Mildred and Irving Levick:

Who can really recount the memories of Sasha? He came to Buffalo often bearing the herring that could be bought only in one place in New York. We'd meet at Mischa's and it was a feast of food and anecdotes. He was a natural! We loved him.

Robert S. Conant:

In December of 1965 there was a subway strike going on at the time of the recording of the Handel Op. 6 concerti for RCA. Transportation was chaotic in town, to say the least, and even getting to the recording was a challenge. Everyone made it in spite of the problems, but not the harpsichord, which was to be delivered by truck from my studio on 57th St. Neither the strike nor gridlock was the reason, but pure human forgetfulness. The mover was mixed up about the time, thinking that we would not record during the strike (an assumption he made on his own). I was mortified and expected both Sasha and RCA to be demanding that I pay for the first session since everyone arrived on time. Sasha was very sympathetic and somehow managed to talk Howard Scott of RCA and the other musicians into rescheduling the session without penalty of any kind on either side. This was truly esprit de corps of the highest sort, and it was only possible with a person like Sasha.

Marc Gottlieb:

Sasha's unstinting enthusiasm for making music and his unshakable belief in the validity of his musical demands have left a profound and everlasting influence on me.

I remember his leadership, his personal devotion and his intense music making during the recordings of the Handel Concerti Grossi at the time of the complete transit strike in NYC. I think that was an unequaled feat of musical endurance!

I also cannot forget the time he held Casals' feet down so they wouldn't "beat" on the recording session!!

Sasha was a once in a lifetime total experience for me and I am proud to have been associated with him for so many years.

Loren Glickman:

I had invited Sasha to my son's bar–mitzvah, but the Budapest Quartet was on tour on the day of the event. On his return, Sasha said to me, "I wanted to get your boy a present, and I thought and thought, what would a thirteen–year–old boy want most of all? And the only thing I could think of was – A Girl –and I didn't know how to get one for him!"

Sasha enjoyed sports, particularly baseball, although he really didn't know the game very well. Each year we would bet 5 dollars on the World Series. And if I lost, Sasha would cackle, gloat, and remind me over and over about how much more knowledgeable he was than I. I paid these gambling losses by check, of course. And Sasha, with much fanfare, would pin the check to our office bulletin board so that all could see, and hear, how smart he was about "bazeball".

One day, I came to meet with him at his apartment. There he was, practicing scales in octaves, thirds, and tenths, while watching a baseball game on television. "Sasha!" I exclaimed in mock horror, "practicing while watching TV?" "Octaves, 3rds, and 10ths are so boring," he replied, "and anyway I can *hear* perfectly well!"

Pamela Gearhart:

By way of brief explanation: during the Budapest's residence at the University of Buffalo (NY), my husband, Livingston Gearhart managed the String Institute which was the precursor of the Christmas String Seminar. The ten day workshop brought talented young string players to Buffalo to work with the quartet and play in the string orchestra conducted by Sasha. During the summer of 1966, as an outgrowth of the String Institute, Livingston organized the Baird Youth Chamber Players. The group rehearsed intensively with Sasha and made two short "tours" which included performances at the Smithsonian and Meadowmount School of Music. The group was sponsored by Mrs. Cameron Baird. The Baird family were close friends as well as mentors of the Budapest and the Schneiders in particular.

During those Buffalo years, I functioned as an "assistant" to Sasha, and as so many, retain a vast store of memories — and remembrances of exhaustion!! One moment perhaps capsulates this complex man. After a particularly intense, frustrating, exasperating, impossible day of travel and rehearsal, during which Sasha had been unreasonably difficult, demanding, and brutal to the students, he stood backstage, about to enter for the concert. He surveyed the attractive group of young string players and said, "Look et dot. Vonderful!! Not one of dem veel ever be a bum!"

Seminar, 1977. Working with students. Photo: Tina Pelikan

David White:

What a man and inspiration!! Priceless playing of his ensembles as he played and conducted, knowing exactly when he had to give more leadership. I also remember trying to help him locate Frank, frantically, at Marlboro when his (Sasha's) car had two flat tires, at the same time!

"Can you connect me with Frank? Where is Frank?" Fortunately we found Frank and all was well. I don't recall who changed the tires, this was in 1965.

Sasha's passing is a great loss to the music world, but his spirit lives on along with the many of his generation who have passed to other worlds. Music unites all worlds.

Elliot Siegel:

It was the night before the first rehearsal of one of the Festival Casals in the 60's. Sasha, Ted Ptashne and I were having dinner in a hotel dining room in San Juan, and were being "entertained" by a violinist of considerable lack of expertise and talent — out of tune, slides to every other note, very wide vibrato. Sasha had his back to the artist. After listening for one minute, he said "This violinist, is he by chance with the Festival Orchestra?" "I don't think so," I replied. Sasha leaned back, heaved a sigh, and whispered "Tenks Gott!"

Jesse Ceci:

On the Marlboro Chamber Orchestra tour in Europe and Israel in August and September of 1965, Sasha was the conductor. One day while most of the orchestra was on the bus waiting for Rudi Serkin, Sasha was seen counting heads in the bus. (I thought he wanted to make sure everyone was on board) Suddenly, he gives out with a scream and says, "Oy vey, we have 22 goyim (gentiles) in the orchestra – such a catastrophe!" Of course this was all done with a sense of humor.

Milton Kestenbaum:

I would say Sasha grabbed life by the throat and wrung it dry. He used every moment of his life.

I remember one year after the Casals Festival, he threw a party at his loft. Bertha and I arrived late and when we got there people were feeling no pain. We approached Sasha who was surrounded by people, and he said "Who wants some vine?" We all agreed and Sasha found some paper cups, opened the bottle and we drank. A man approached, his face aghast and purple, saying, "Sasha, what are you doing?" Sasha replied, "We are drinking the vine." "But Sasha," the man replied, "that wine was a special present for you, I paid $1,000 for that bottle!"

"So what," replied Sasha, "so we are drinking the vine!"

Wherever Sasha is now, he is drinking $1,000 bottles of "vine" out of paper cups.

Thomas Suárez:

The first memory to share with you is of an impromptu lesson Sasha gave me in 1966 at an auditorium in Buffalo, on the slow movement of the a minor Bach violin concerto. If seemingly mundane in itself, two things were remarkable about this coaching. Firstly, during the course of the unscheduled 1+ hour that he spent with me on the one movement, a sizable audience gradually assembled, attracted not because of my playing but rather because of Sasha's enthusiasm. Secondly, although he mercilessly micro–

59

scrutinized my interpretation of the movement, he did so in such a way that it made the lesson (and of course the music) more exciting rather than laborious and "studied" and made me more in command and confident, rather than making me terrified and self–conscious. There is the fable about the caterpillar who, at the request of a curious spider, tries to explain how he walks with so many legs, but in doing so tediously analyzes the question to the point that he himself can no longer even move, being psychologically crippled. Sasha's genius was to tear apart every nuance of every note without crippling me.

The second memory I would like to relate is more unusual. At the very first New York seminar, I approached Sasha a day before the Carnegie Hall concert and suggested that we dedicate one of the works on the program (I believe it was the Barber "Adagio") to the effort against the Vietnam war. He was enthusiastic about the idea. So I prepared a short speech stating that we, being Mr. Schneider and the orchestra (the orchestra seemed to offer tacit approval) wished to perform the following work in the hopes of world peace and of an end to the US. military involvement in Indochina. He had me walk up to the front of the stage before the performance of the piece to make the speech to the audience.

To appreciate this event, you must remember that it was still at a time when such a position was not openly "acceptable," and that Sasha left himself open to criticism and other repercussions for getting involved with it. I, of course had proposed and carried out the idea out of blind adolescent brazenness, but Sasha allowed me to do it out of a conviction and integrity that many other "famous" people did not risk. Most people in his position would not have allowed a then–controversial political twist to muddle a nonpolitical artistic endeavor, particularly a new and vulnerable one, as it was sure to annoy some audience and sponsors. It clearly says a lot about him that he risked such a gesture, and in fact did so without hesitation. He instead could have reasonably argued that he was sympathetic to the idea, but that it was inappropriate. I believe that in its own small way, the incident contributed to the eventual demise of the government's myth that such dissension was "extremist".

Sonata recital with the very young Murray Perahia, now a world renowned pianist. Photo: T. Suárez

June Becera:

Sasha was a good friend and we loved him. My late husband and I first met Sasha when the Festival Casals started here in Puerto Rico in 1956 and we continued that friendship all these years.

While Sasha was in Puerto Rico for the Festival – the 6 day war (1967) started. For the next concert to be given after the start of the war Sasha changed the program for the Festival and was very busy – so he could not go sailing with my husband. To cheer Sasha up, I had a small cake made for him with the first few notes of Beethoven's Fifth Symphony put on the frosting, and sent it to his hotel. He was very touched!! But that is not the end of the story. Sasha took the cake to N.Y. and displayed it framed on the wall for a long time. Then he put it in the freezer for many, many months – and forgot about it. Later he found the cake and served it at a dinner for dessert. Needless to say all his guests asked "What is this?!" Sasha told me this with great glee and laughter. He could laugh with himself and at himself. We shall miss him.

Don Stewart:

During my summers at Marlboro 1966, 67, 68, I didn't get to know Sasha much at all: never in the same groups. But I observed etc. Then, one night about two years later, I chanced to be in the same subway car with Sasha, from around Carnegie Hall to 23rd St. (I had a loft on 21st at this time). I reintroduced myself to him and we began to chatter about the tough life of a musician etc. He allowed that things were a bit more livable in London, etc. Soon we were at 23rd and got off together. I knew he had a place in the neighborhood, but I didn't know it was right close. He invited me in, and of course I accepted. We talked for maybe two hours over, if memory serves, a good white wine and excellent leftovers. Very pleasant. He didn't really know me, and I wasn't a string player who specialized in 19th century music. So, his humanity and generosity was most apparent and welcome. NYC wasn't really treating me especially well during this time. I never saw him or worked with him again. We talked of music and life. Nice.

Ruth Laredo:

When my daughter, Jennifer Alexandra was born in 1969 (the Alexandra was for Sasha), he came over a few days after we had brought her home from the hospital. Sasha seemed truly moved, subdued, even quiet in the presence of the baby. (How unusual for such a high–voltage personality!) He had brought a gift for her. Under his arm, he had been carrying a parcel wrapped in ordinary brown paper. Unfolding it gently, Sasha revealed a layer of cloth, and then the contents, which glinted of gold and mother–of–pearl.

But these were not jewels! Sasha had lovingly assembled a collection of priceless gold and silver knives, forks and spoons with elegant mother–of–pearl handles from "the old country." Such was his baby gift to my daughter.

It was all the more touching because Sasha had given Jennifer something utterly personal and irreplaceable in one intimate gesture.

The Cleveland Quartet:

We will all remember Sasha for his inspirational artistry, his generosity, enthusiasm, his never ending energy, love of life and his subtle sense of humor (schmoekedores not excluded...).

About 25 years ago, in Blue Hill, Maine, at a post–concert reception, we were all waiting anxiously for Sasha's critique of one of our first performances. Glancing over our shoulders at a magnificent white salmon, his first words were: "Terrific playing, but if you want to be a professional quartet, you have to learn to eat. Let's go!"

We will miss him.

Jesse Ceci:

During the Casals Festival in San Juan, some members of the orchestra were showing Sasha the nudes and centerfold of Playboy magazine. He looked at them for a moment and said "This is only a piece of paper – give me the real ting!"

Richard Woodhams:

I played with Alexander Schneider in St. Louis many times between 1970 and 1977. He conducted a chamber orchestra comprised of members of the St. Louis Symphony and he also played chamber music with us.

I'm sure that many other people have vivid recollections of his colorful and vital personality (my favorite phrase was "Don't do dot, Ja?") but in addition, what I will always remember was the ability he had to get absolutely the most musical meaning from Haydn Symphonies. His imagination led him, by varying his bow technique, its speed and placement and distribution, to get many different timbres from a string section by demonstrating for them the possibilities of the musical expression. And, for me, the expression was absolutely right for the music, and the sounds he came up with originated from the music rather than vice–versa. I loved it and will miss it but always will remember it.

I was saddened to hear of Sasha's death but I must say that as I sit writing this letter thinking of all my experiences with him, both good and even not always so good, I smile because I feel enriched by having known and played with him.

So, I smile out of respect and love, with wonderful memories of his joyful music–making.

Christine Reed:

I have countless recollections of experiences with Sasha but most of them are unprintable! I have always felt somehow privileged to have had the opportunity to work so closely with him for so long and to have been privy to all facets of his remarkable personality. I've kept all his letters, cards, notes, etc. since we met in 1970 and in them I've been able over the years to hang onto all of the wonderful (and painful) memories he gave me.

Working for Sasha in my early twenties, right out of college, was both a blessing and a curse. He was larger than life — determined to experience everyone and everything in the extreme. He used to lecture me about how I (being a "Midwest milkmaid") had to develop more temperament! In the beginning, it was all I could do to understand his accent much less comprehend that directive. But over time, I learned some very essential and valuable lessons from him that have been irreplaceable throughout my entire life. I learned to have a curiosity and appreciation for every minute of life, to expect the most from people and situations and especially, myself, to have a passion for music and no patience for inflated egos. I learned loyalty and caring and creativity and style. I learned how to cook, appreciate fine wine and much about art. I also learned how not to dress and above all, to maintain my tranquility if at all possible!

65

The difficulty in being given such gifts so young was that I was spoiled for life! Never again would I be exposed to anyone of comparable integrity or lack of guile in my professional career. There was a purity of spirit about Sasha that no other human being I have ever met (with exception of my mother) has possessed. Working for and with him was nothing if not challenging and yet endlessly rewarding. Every experience I have had since then has been a compromise to the standards he set. Even long after I worked for him he would still "give me over the head" if he thought I needed it and usually, underneath all the "hazerie" of his bombast, there was a thread of truth from which to learn. He was a loyal and generous source of guidance and friendship to me until the day he died. There will never be anyone to replace Sasha in my life and I'll always miss him but I'm sure he's found "Schmoekedores" heaven and is busy making his inimitable music and "michugas".

Stephanie Brown:

I vividly remember the bewilderment I felt at my first rehearsal with Sasha. We were playing a Haydn trio, and soon I began hearing, "Phrase! Phrase! PHRASE!" Then a little louder — "You're not phrasing!" Still louder, "Pianists never phrase! They don't know how to phrase!" I thought to myself, "But what does he mean? I am phrasing. I do know how to phrase."

To Sasha, "phrasing" meant something very different from the usual meaning of following a musical line up and down and articulating its various points of tension and relaxation. To him, phrasing was synonymous with "making music," and making music meant, simply, putting every atom of your musical being into every note. Anything less was a sacrilege, and earned Sasha's ultimate insult: "You sound like a true professional."

At a certain point in every rehearsal, however, he would lean back in his chair, at last able to relax, smiling and satisfied — and say, "Now, finally, you understand. Now you don't sound like a pianist. Now you're phrasing!" — his highest compliment.

Whatever I played with Sasha left an indelible impression in my mind. In fact, I cannot hear certain phrases of Haydn Trios or Brahms Quartets without hearing them just the way Sasha used to play them, with every nuance, every unique bite of the bow, and every heightened intonation perfectly intact.

For Sasha, music was always the most beautiful part of a day. We would rehearse all morning, stop to eat lunch prepared by him — a beef stew, his favorite bread, an excellent bottle (or two, or three) of wine — and then rehearse for the rest of the afternoon, telling stories all the way. The concept of music as "work" would have been impossible for Sasha to comprehend. Music was, simply, the greatest pleasure of life, and being a musician, life's greatest privilege.

There were many irreverent moments. I remember one particular Schubert Trout dress rehearsal. Sasha was telling stories all through the rehearsal — how he'd played the piece hundreds of times, with so many different players, and how every single time, no matter where he'd played it, the audience would applaud at the D major cadence in the middle of the last movement.

Then suddenly, I remember, his eyes lit up. "No, it's enough," he said. "Tonight is going to be different. I'm tired of them always clapping in the middle of the last movement. Tonight, if I hear a single clap, the concert is over." Then louder, "Not another note!" Even louder —"If those Schmoekedores don't BY NOW know the Trout Quintet, they don't deserve to hear the whole piece."

He was delighted with his plan. Backstage before the concert, he whispered conspiratorially to all of us, "Don't

67

forget, not another note." It was very hard to concentrate, wondering through the whole piece what was going to happen in the last movement — whether Sasha would really go through with it, because the one thing that was not in question, of course, was whether the audience would clap in the middle of the last movement.

Finally we came to the tumbling run, leading into the fateful D major chord. I watched as Sasha made a huge flourish with his bow and turned expectantly toward the audience, waiting for the applause...

Dead quiet. Not a single clap. The silence was deafening. Finally, with a loud and disgusted sigh, Sasha gave the cue for the next note, a single unison B ... which had five distinct entrances. We finished the movement, and after the concert, his joke ruined, Sasha kept muttering to himself, "The only time ... as many times as I've played this piece ... my whole life I played the piece ... why this night, OF ALL NIGHTS ... they don't clap?"

Steve Ansell:

I will remember Sasha for his great energy and generosity of spirit, but first and foremost for his ability to communicate his deepest feelings for the music that we cherish, that keeps us all young, and binds us with its life. Always in my memory will be the time in 1971 at the Christmas Seminar when, with Sasha's guidance and strong exhortations, we attempted to plumb the depths of the slow movement of Op. 135, which as youngsters we could not possibly understand. Only years later did I realize what he had been trying to get us to see and feel. This became one of the defining moments of my entire musical education, and I will always be deeply indebted to him for it. The spirit of music lived in Sasha, and both his spirit and that of the music will live on in those he touched. God bless him.

ALEXANDER SCHNEIDER
5 EAST 20TH STREET
NEW YORK. N. Y. 10003
(212) CA 8-2980

I dont write Postcards!
a letter is more expensive
and I love to give you some
food & Wine, so call me &
I don't need a JOB

Sasha.

Oct. 17
Just back from
Europe & Japan!

69

Catherine Lehr:

I was part of the Christmas String Seminar in 1972 and 73. We had orchestra for nine hours a day and after that would read chamber music long into the night. It was tremendously exciting for me. One of the things I remember about Sasha Schneider is that he was always making fun of the old orchestra musicians who sat back in the string section, didn't care about or listen to the music, and according to Sasha were just waiting to collect their pensions. When he made these comments at the string seminar, no one was offended (we were all under the age of 22). However, in 1975 I joined the St. Louis Symphony, and when Sasha came to conduct and sprinkled his comments with nasty remarks about old musicians waiting to collect their pensions, some of my colleagues were definitely not amused.

I have now been a part of the orchestra musicians world for eighteen years, and am some 20 years closer to collecting my own pension than when I first met Sasha Schneider. Fortunately, in the orchestra in which I play there are very few of the uncaring, cynical orchestra musicians that Sasha was so fond of denigrating. But certainly all of us in the music business know such musicians. I think that having known Sasha, with his lifelong enthusiasm for music, has left me better prepared to age gracefully in my profession, to continually find the music fresh and exciting. He helped lay the foundation for my own love of playing in an ensemble. How sad that he is no longer with us.

Laurie Smukler:

Sasha was a profound influence in my life for many years. But he was really the hero of my adolescence and young adulthood. My young questing heart found in him the embodiment of passion, musical vision, commitment and energy. My first Christmas Seminar, under his direction, gave me as a fifteen year old the prototype of how life should be lived with driving force to obtain the best in it – whether the object of desire was companionship, a glass of wine, or the perfect phrase. It was electrifying to be personally under his command, to be driven both by his storms and his love to reach past where I had ever reached before.

In the two Christmas Seminars I participated in, as well as during Brandenburg Ensemble and the intermittent coachings Sasha gave my fledgling quartet, I was not only fortunate enough to share in his musical life, but I also got to glimpse his personal life as well. It is from his personal life that I would like to share a special memory.

I was twenty–one or so, living the wonderful life of almost not a student. I got a call from Frank Salomon. Would I please come and stay in their home while they were away? Misha would be in New York staying at their apartment and they really would feel better if someone were there at night and to get him his breakfast in the morning. Would I ever! I was honored. And by the way, the second night I was to be there, Sasha had orchestrated an event for his brother that I would be included in. Was I in for an experience! The time I spent with Misha was very special, among other things he taught me how to make a decent cup of coffee. But the evening was about as colorful as it could be and it was all because of Sasha. This was it – Sasha and Misha (and I, by default) were to be special guests of Zero Mostel at his performance of "Fiddler on the Roof." Sasha, I gathered was great friends with Zero Mostel and wanted to share that friendship, and Mostel's great performance with his beloved brother. He set up the evening by having Misha and I picked up in a beautiful black chauffeured limousine. This was not the way Sasha traveled – he wanted this for his brother. We got in, both surprised, but Misha smiled, looked proud, and said in his most elegant but heavily accented voice, "Just drive!" When we got to the theater, Sasha met us and helped

Sasha with Jack Benny. Photo: T. Suárez

his brother in, walking slowly for Misha but also for the grandeur of it. He proudly introduced him to many acquaintances, jokingly called me Misha's date and in general made a very happy scene. When we finally sat in our seats the brothers sat together and I next to Misha. The performance, for me, was filled with many wonderful things. The show was great. I loved the story and the music. But being privy to the interaction between Sasha, his brother and his friend was equally special to me. Mostel acknowledged Sasha and his brother from the stage, and directed a great many of his lines in our direction. Sasha and Misha whispered a great deal, laughed together, and obviously shared deeply the poignancy of the story. I was awed thinking of these three great men, all Jews, all getting older, all sharing some part of a common history that was the theme of the very play we were watching. And I was awed by the performer performing for the performers, and how very much it meant to all of them.

When the performance was over, there was little time allowed for sentiment. Sasha bustled us to the front of the theater, up a few tiny steps to the stage and plunk into Mostel's offstage dressing room. If you could call it a dressing room. It was a tiny space and Zero Mostel's beaming costumed countenance seemed to be taking up all of it. However, we squeezed in, a seat was found for Misha, and the merriment began. Compliments were given round, Mostel was deferential to Misha, there was much leg slapping hilarity in Yiddish, which I couldn't understand. It seemed that I would escape unnoticed until Sasha presented me quite soundly and Mostel asked my name. It was a great moment for Sasha. "Her name is Laurie Schmoekedores!" Well, he was close enough to make it hilarious and make me scarlet with embarrassment – which of course only increased all three men's enjoyment. After that moment I was included. We stayed briefly, and they talked of people and times that they shared. Then Sasha became concerned about Misha's fatigue level so we said our good–byes. Graciously, Mostel suggested we use the actor's exit from the theater – there were less steps for Misha. Sasha thought that was grand. As we exited Sasha took one of Misha's arms and suggested that I take the other. So situated, we made our way from the theater. As we stepped out, the fans waiting outside started to clap. Of course, they were expecting Zero Mostel to step out – that's who they were waiting for – but the funny thing was, they seemed perfectly happy to clap for Sasha and Misha and whoever that young girl was who was with them. Sasha gave me a huge smile, winked and said in his thick Russian accent "Just walk!" So we did – all enjoying our escorted parade to the waiting limousine. Sasha kissed his brother on both cheeks, then me, chuckling, "Oh,

Sasha with Rudolf Serkin, world famous pianist, at a recording session. January 1956.

you Schmoekedores!" And we left him. He probably walked home as we swept back to Frank's in our sleek limousine.

Later that night as I tried unsuccessfully to get to sleep, I called Ira, to try to talk about how much this evening – with Sasha, Misha, and Mostel had meant to me. It seemed impossible then, and still does, but, sharing it now in the context of gathering remembrances of Sasha, I hope it can add to the whole – as we celebrate the enormous being and experience he was for all of us.

David Soyer :

"The goddam doctors killed Zero Mostel!"

"What do you mean, Sasha, the doctors killed Mostel?"

"Zero ate too much, drank too much, smoked too much,

and made love too much. Then the doctors told him to cut down on everything. Vell, he did – – – and he died! The goddam doctors killed Zero Mostel!!"

Molly King:

In the season of 1972–1973, I worked for New School Concerts (with the Christmas String Seminar) and Festival Casals, so I was fairly familiar with Sasha's renowned curmudgeonly, rather autocratic ways.

That February, Sasha had turned 65, and in the fall, a number of his friends and colleagues were at a birthday celebration at his home on 20th Street. Sasha was cooking and enjoying his role as host; people were laughing and having great fun.

Late in the evening a telephone call came in which Sasha received the news of the death of Pablo Casals. The mood of the party changed instantly. Sasha became very quiet, his pain obvious. After a short while, he was able to speak and he told all of us, in the most tender and poignant way, stories and expressions of his love and respect for the cello master.

It was a side of Sasha few of us had seen, and I will always remember that sad, special evening. It added a whole new dimension to my perception of him, and I felt I had become acquainted with the "real" Sasha.

Jane Dugan Baird:

At Baird parties there were skits. One was a trial of Mischa as a male chauvinist. One of Mischa's favorite questions was "Why aren't there any famous women composers?" The prosecutor produced one that day. Yes it was Alex – at his craziest best – dressed as a woman in a wig, hat, and dress. The prosecutor won the case!! Great memories...

Sasha at party arguing for women's rights. Photo: Jane Dugan Baird.

Gerard Schwarz:

Quite a number of years ago, probably 1974 or 75, I was doing a tour of the Northeast with Sasha Schneider and the Brandenburg Ensemble. The tour ended at Dartmouth College in New Hampshire in a wonderful little hall, and the concert was marvelous. I asked Sasha if he would like to have something to eat after the concert. I was flying back to New York the next morning and I assumed he was too.

He said , "No, there is a midnight train from Dartmouth." He was planning to take the train to New York. I said, "Gee, that's a terrible thing. You could relax after the concert, have a glass of wine and a nice dinner, go to sleep and we could fly back in the morning. It would be much easier."

He said, "No, you don't understand, tomorrow is a big day for me." Of course, I inquired why this was so important. Well, it turned out that a girlfriend from Texas (I think) was coming in to have lunch with him and another girlfriend from elsewhere was coming to have dinner with him that night.

He said, "You know, I'm not as young as I used to be — I don't know what I am going to do with one girlfriend in the afternoon and another in the evening. I am just very nervous."

Knowing Sasha as we all do, I could understand his apprehension. But off he went.

The next day, I heard this terrible story about how Sasha lost his great violin in a taxicab at the conclusion of the train trip. It was either by Guarneri or Stradivari. He arrived in New York at Grand Central Station, grabbed a cab to go to his brownstone on 20th Street, and left the violin in the taxi. There was a big to–do about it — rewards were offered and it was on the news. There was considerable attention given to the loss of this extremely valuable instrument.

Everyone who was friendly with Sasha called him and expressed their concern. It was much like the loss of a child. I was actually rather embarrassed for him. Imagine what it would be like losing an instrument of such value, not only financial but also musical. Personally, I would crawl under a table and hope no one would notice I had done such a thing. So, a propos of my own reasoning, I felt all these people calling him must be a burden on him. I decided not to be among those people causing further distress; I would simply leave the poor man alone and not call him at all.

Eventually, the violin was found and everything turned out just fine. I saw Sasha about six months later and he said to me, "Jerry, I am not speaking to you." I responded, "Sasha, why? What did I do wrong? Why aren't you speaking to me?" He said, "You didn't call me when I lost my fiddle." I explained to him why I didn't call. He said, "No, you are the only one who knew the real reason why I lost my fiddle."

. . . and that's the end of the story.

Betsy Schulberg:

I had known Sasha for many years, and when I heard that Maria Callas was making her comeback in a concert at Carnegie Hall, I called him and suggested that we go together.

Soon after the concert started, Sasha left his seat. In the intermission I found him pacing up and down the lobby of the theater. When I asked him what was wrong, he said, "I can't take it — I can't! She is so off pitch it hurts my ears!"

I wanted to hear the rest of the concert, so Sasha waited for me outside, the perfectionist musician and the perfect gentleman.

William Xucla:

My most vivid and impressive recollection of Alexander "Sasha" Schneider is, oddly, not of his music making or his humor (both of which I loved) but of his moral courage and integrity.

It was December of 1979, on Don Pablo's birthday, that a special church service was held in old San Juan. Its significance was the transferring of Casals' body from Puerto Rico back to his native Catalunya, satisfying the Maestro's lifelong desire to return to his native homeland once democracy had been restored.

The brief program had an air about it of something that seemed to be hastily put together: from the cello on the altar (that was not Casals' beloved Bergonzi–Goffriller) to the music (a perfunctory reading of Bach's Air On The G String by my orchestra, the Puerto Rico Symphony), to the very end of the program. Ah, yes, the end of the program was one of those incidents in life that exposes a man's soul: carelessly (or deliberately, for I found out to my amazement, that the Puerto Ricans detested Casals) someone put on a tape of Casals playing the "Cant D'Ocells" in reverse, to the end of the ceremony. Of course, it sounded something like Alban Berg. From my vantage point in the Bass section, I could see only the faces of Martita Casals and Governor Barcelo and his political cronies in the front row. Whispers abounded until we all realized what had happened. Governor Barcelo and his friends had a belly laugh, Martita and most of us on stage were in shock and at a loss as to what to do. But one man (who had been out of my line of sight) suddenly came into view with a look of outraged anger on his face and with a few quick strides was at the edge of the stage. Alexander Schneider promptly and wordlessly stretched out his arms to our concertmaster Pepito Figueroa, who unhesitatingly yielded his Strad to "Sasha," who then rendered a gorgeous "Song of the Birds" in honor of his beloved Don Pablo and to the shame of those who lacked his moral backbone.

Casals Festival rehearsal, Puerto Rico, late 1950's. Sasha with Pablo Casals and Isaac Stern. Photo: L. Glickman

Ramon C. Bolpata:

I always thought that I would have time to thank Alexander Schneider for his kindness and his patronage, and acknowledge the many things he taught me. It is perhaps a testament to his youthfulness that as the years passed by, I never realized that his remaining time with us was short. The imperative to give thanks and celebrate the largesse of a benefactor only arises, I'm afraid, when it seems to do least good, to have least effect. For though I celebrate and acknowledge the favor of a great man, the words are truly for his ears alone, and he cannot hear them. I can only hope that he is here, watching his friends at concert, and thus hear me.

I first met Sasha almost 15 years ago when auditioning for the Christmas String Seminar in New York. He then picked me for the Seminar, to play at Carnegie. Later, Sasha made me his principal cellist in the Brandenburg Ensemble, and we toured together for many years. Sasha helped launch my professional life.

In those years on tour, Sasha taught me numerous things about poise, showmanship, professionalism. Some of those I was old enough to absorb at the time. Some I am only now learning. But all of them, the punctuality, the respect, the perfectionism of the great musician, I learned in large part to what I saw during those ten years with a great man who knew the great traditions of musical performance. Not just the art, but the craft.

Good–bye Sasha, and thank you. Take excellent good care of yourself.

Fritz Gearhart:

To this day, the energy and vitality of Sasha's music–making reverberates in my brain. I now conduct a small string orchestra at East Carolina University. I hope I am able to give 1/1000th of the energy to my students, that he gave me. I will never forget him saying ". . . it is such a pri–vil–ege to make music", I can hear his distinctive rhythmic emphasis on every word, feel the intensity of his eyes, the undying completeness of his devotion to our Art.

David Lennon:

Sasha meant so much to so many different people. Although the list of his selfless and dedicated accomplishments far exceed most any man's in a lifetime, he will especially be remembered by many as Master Teacher.

Although my experience in the New York String Orchestra seminars took place well over ten years ago,

81

Sasha's gifts have stayed with me long after my last concert with him. His New York String Orchestra seminar was not merely a gathering of fine young and aspiring musicians preparing a series of concerts together. Although we had the basic ingredients to go on to be fine instrumentalists, it was Alexander Schneider who breathed life and meaning into the very essence of who we were and could be as musicians in society. Over the past decade I have witnessed this in careers that took various directions, whether it was those of us whose talents would best serve as soloists, chamber or orchestral musicians. It wasn't the form of giving he emphasized, rather the honest and deep connection to the heart that he invoked in each and every one of us.

I could count dozens of encounters with seminar alumni over the years who share the bond of what we learned and would take with us far beyond those precious ten days one December long ago.

I believe Sasha's greatest gift to us was his profound wisdom and understanding that only in the spirit of genuine giving can we as musicians and human beings truly receive. The miracle of his teaching was just that. Music making from the purest source within him as his expression of love to all of us. May he be blessed in eternity as we whose lives he touched.

Robert F. Hoffman:

I have two stories about Sasha, a rather droll one and another with more significance.

I've known Sasha since I was in high school. Toward the end of my college years I decided to grow a beard. (Razors are dangerous first thing in the morning!) When he first saw my beginning stubble, Sasha clucked disapprovingly, "Ze girls von't kiss you." For years, whenever

I saw him he called me "Barbudo" but was always dubious when I reassured him that the beard seemed to have no adverse effect on my romantic life.

The first time I ever worked with Sasha was at the University of Buffalo during a Spring vacation seminar for high school students. I was the only bassist in a string orchestra of 40 or more. I was rather overawed by the experience of learning from Sasha and the other members of the Budapest Quartet then in residence (Mischa and Boris), whose 78rpm's of the Beethoven Quartets I treasured. Mezzo piano was the loudest I could muster in my nervousness. At one point, Sasha stopped the rehearsal and said to me, "You play in tune, play louder!"

That sentence had a bracing effect on me, especially after the break when second timers told me Sasha's compliments were not given lightly. His encouragement gave my confidence just the boost it needed and I went on to play enthusiastically not just then but also in a tour with Sasha the following summer and later as the principal bassist of the first and second annual Christmas string seminars.

The most vital thing I took away from working with Sasha was that music should never be taken for granted. Every note counts. Every note and phrase has its place and should be played thoughtfully, emotionally, and with commitment.

It is in large measure because of Sasha — his confidence in me (and thus mine in myself) and his commitment to making music and not just playing notes — that I became a professional musician.

Epilogue: : Alas, there are not enough Sashas in the world. A decade of free–lancing, of uncommitted music making, of insufficient rehearsing, of music as simply a job and not a joy, finally took its toll. Sasha set a standard and it became impossible to endure anything less.

Charles Haupt:

Sasha would come to Buffalo regularly to conduct string orchestra concerts. During his next to last visit I played the Bach Double with Charles Castleman and the Bach E+ Concerto myself. After one of the rehearsals Willa Rouder, our concert manager, drove him to his hotel. Keeping in mind that Sasha had known me since I was a kid the following is all the stranger for it.

During the drive Sasha with his usual hyperbole told Willa that after Jaime Laredo, I was his favorite gentile violinist. Willa described the exchange as follows:

"But, Sasha. Charlie is Jewish."

"Vat you talking about."

"Charles isn't gentile, Sasha. He's Jewish."

"Him? Jewish? Impossible! I know him twenty years."

"Believe me, Sasha, he's Jewish. Why is it impossible?"

A pregnant pause.

Sputtering as only Sasha could sputter he finally responded:

"But is impossible! Because..... because he has GOYIM CHUTZPA!"

Sasha's passing is a great loss for all of us and especially for music which was, after all, his great comrade, lover and plaything.

Arlene Gould:

In 1982, Sasha was invited to be guest conductor at the Hudson Valley Philharmonic, where I was then Director of Public Relations. Since I was aware of Sasha's cataract operations, I volunteered to be his eyes and hostess during the week he was in the Hudson Valley. This proved to be an unforgettable time for me. We had lots of time to talk. It was incredibly exciting (because up until this time Sasha

84

had never paid any attention to me and had only grunted orders at me.) So, I got to be chauffeur, tour guide and general factotum. I took him to the best restaurants I could find, and the best of the Hudson Valley wineries. We had conversations about the pros and cons of the institution of marriage (he was generally con!) and music, literature, politics, arts, current events, Israel, food and of course wine.

We actually got to know each other a bit as human beings. I think he liked the idea that I was part Litvak! He complained about all kinds of things, including Frank Salomon's insistence that he continue conducting the String Seminar and the Brandenburg Ensemble. (I think he knew he could complain to me because he knew that I agreed with Frank and felt that he still had lots left to give.) He harangued the Hudson Valley Philharmonic, but got them to play with more spirit and verve than even they knew they had. I will always treasure that week I spent with Sasha. I think he had a good time too, because thereafter, when I would see him on Christmas Eves at Carnegie Hall or at The New School, he'd grab me in his bear–hug and say, "I should have married you thirty years ago!"

Sidney Long:

Although I did not meet Sasha until he was 75, I made up for lost time because for nine months I served as his ghostwriter (1983–1984). It was a great privilege to pore over his fabulous collection of photographs, read his correspondence (much of it from young musicians whose lives he had changed), and go through the 20th century with him, from Vilna to Berlin to Paris to San Francisco to New York to Jerusalem. By the time it was over I felt that I had *become* Sasha, a state from which it was not easy to recover. Sasha was truly larger than life, but I suspect he would say

85

that life is large and most people don't live up to it. His exuberance was legendary, but he also had a thoughtful, introspective side that balanced the laughter and drama. We had a great time together, but unfortunately he was disappointed with the results of our collaboration, as was I. But I had a better idea than he what went wrong. There were two Sashas. One Sasha was extremely candid with a deep understanding of human nature and an honest appraisal of his own failings and disappointments, the other Sasha was concerned with promulgating a certain image of himself both as a man and as a musician. As a result much of the fascinating material narrated to me by the first Sasha was later disavowed or disallowed by the second. When I heard the expression, "but this is not me" my heart would sink because I knew that another memory was going to be severely edited. It was frustrating, but it was also fascinating to see both sides so clearly. He was a marvelous man, he made a great impression on my life, and I will always be grateful that I got to know him.

June Becera:

Eight years ago (1985) my grandson, violinist Christian Colberg was to audition at Peabody Conservatory. Shortly before the scheduled auditions, Sasha made a trip to Puerto Rico. At a private dinner at my apartment he heard Christian playing and offered to lend him one of his own violins – I believe it was Vuillaume – for the audition. We passed through New York on our way to Baltimore and picked up the valuable violin. Christian was accepted at Peabody.

The above illustrates Sasha's interest always in young musicians, and his desire to help them with great generosity.

Jeff Keesecker:

I participated in the New York String Seminar in December of 1984. I am very happy to have the opportunity to pay my respects by making this contribution, however small, to "Celebrating Sasha."

That Christmas in 1984 was a seminal one for me. I learned so much in such a short time from Mr. Schneider. So many things he mentioned, both about the music and away from it, have stayed with me to this day, and I expect I will never forget them. While I would never consider myself a friend of his (I'm sure he never even knew my name), he had such a profound effect on my musical being (which he also never knew).

First of all, I remember the music. We were playing Brahms, and in the first rehearsal he pulled his violin straight away, and started showing us the phrasing he was looking for in all the parts, not just the violins. Suddenly a new world opened up for me. It was so simple the way he accomplished it: he just sang and played the phrases, so beautifully and with such nuance, I had never seen or heard anything like it, and it seemed so perfect for Brahms. I have never forgotten it, and I think back to this phrasing every time I play Brahms or anything like it. Not just in the back of my mind, but the front of it. I have always felt most in tune with Romantic period music, and this experience provided me a new vocabulary, opened my eyes and let me look into Brahms' heart and music the way I'm sure I would not have done without Sasha's influence.

I remember during the seminar, he needed someone to apartment sit for him while he went to a rehearsal or something. Some repairman or some such was coming and there was a need for someone to meet him. Those details are not important. A friend of mine and me (both of us were the bassoonists in the orchestra) were asked to do the job

87

and we agreed readily. What a gallery his place was! It was an old place down in the 20's as I remember, a big loft. Very eclectic furnishing style, complete with a rack of seats (we found out later) from the original Metropolitan Opera. It was literally wallpapered with photographs. My friend and I looked at every one I think, trying to figure out who were all the people in the pictures, and there were a lot of them. It was a fun challenge and occupied the day. We also watched a ridiculous black and white videotape starring Jascha Heifetz, where he carried on his daily business, over and under acting badly along the way, and then would suddenly give an impromptu violin recital, playing stunningly. It even included a visual effect of Heifetz's fingers in slow motion, with no sound. The playing was exquisite, of course, but I could have done without the periphery. We were told later it was Sasha's favorite film and he watched it religiously. I also remember a great note pad for messages which I have not seen since, and for all I know, was custom–made. It was a beautifully curved drawing of a man on top of a woman, making love, with the caption on the top, "Things to do today." Unique.

When the orchestra was rehearsing in Carnegie Hall, he said something I have also never forgotten. The back of the orchestra was having trouble seeing him as he conducted. It was apparently his habit to conduct from the floor, rather than a podium. When it was suggested that he use a podium, he replied, "I am not a conductor, I am a musician!" The remark was greeted with enthusiastic applause from the orchestra.

He also made it possible for me to do the kind of thing most people don't get a chance to do: play in Carnegie Hall. It was all great, and I keep it all with me forever.

Sasha, the bassoon virtuoso. 1950's

Arlene Gould:

Perhaps my most unusual "Sasha Story" did not involve Sasha at all, directly that is. It started during the summer of 1984 when I was having a happy hour cocktail with Mischa at Marlboro. "So, what's new?" he asked me, as always. I told him I was planning a trip to Australia in December. He then insisted that I call an old friend and say hello for him. I said, of course I would. The old friend turned out to be Gerde Meyer, Sasha's first wife. She lived in Melbourne and had recently retired from teaching German literature at the university. Mischa had introduced them in the early 1930's in Germany. She and Sasha had had a tempestuous and short marriage. Gerde decided she did not want to be a "quartet wife" and left Sasha. She went as far away as she could get – Australia! During the ensuing years she and Mischa stayed in touch.

So, on December 26th, Boxing Day in Australia, I called Gerde from my hotel in Melbourne with greetings from Mischa Schneider. Well, she was thrilled to hear from her old friend. She wanted to know who I was and insisted that I, (and my mother, with whom I was travelling) come right over to her home for tea that afternoon. She wanted to know all about Sasha and Mischa and to trade stories. A most delightful, gracious, compact, vivacious and intelligent woman welcomed us. We chatted for hours, ate delicious cakes and traded news and stories. She told us how she had certainly fallen for Sasha after Mischa introduced them. But that after the 'round the world tour with the quartet (during which she first discovered Australia) and then the constant travelling, Gerde decided Sasha was not the kind of husband she wanted after all. Besides, she said, they fought all the time! Anyway, she recollected, they were both opinionated and headstrong, so it just wasn't going to work.

The worst part of the situation for Gerde was that her mother adored Sasha and couldn't understand why she was not happy in the marriage. Sasha was bruised and angry at Gerde, but he stayed friends with her mother in Europe. This made the relationship between Gerde and her mother difficult. In those days, girls didn't just up and leave their husbands! At any rate, Gerde left around 1937 and moved to Australia where she eventually remarried and became a professor of German Literature at the University. I didn't find out if she'd had any children, but she said she had a very happy and busy life in Melbourne, which is a cultivated and sophisticated city. On her periodic visits to New York she would call Mischa and eventually she even saw Sasha, but not often. Of course, she wished them all well and I promised to give them her love. Needless to say, we had a great afternoon and meeting her showed me a new dimension of Sasha. He was always attracted to independent, energetic and headstrong women.

Loren Glickman:

Sasha was the essence of the macho man, not posing or bragging, but in truth the lover of many women. His conversation was peppered with allusions to love, women, sex, and the pleasures therein. So, naturally, over the years, I have many recollections of Sasha in that vein.

In the early years of the Casals Festival in Puerto Rico, before the advent of jets, the trip used to take over six hours. On one occasion, after everyone was settled, and Sasha had greeted each musician and spent a little time with each, he started a flirtation with a lovely young airline stewardess. Off and on, for six hours, he romanced this sweet girl, and shortly before we were to land in San Juan, Sasha got around to suggesting they go out on a date that very evening. "I can't," she replied. "I promised to go out with Peter" (a cellist in the orchestra). Exasperated, Sasha exclaimed

"When did you promise?" "As soon as the trip began," she answered brightly.

At one of his huge parties, I noticed a beautiful young girl of about 18 who seemed to be hanging on his every word, as well as his arm and shoulders. (Sasha was well into his seventies at the time.) The following day, I called to tell him how much we had enjoyed the party. Then I asked if the lovely young girl had stayed the night with him. He said she had. I asked if he had enjoyed her "company". Sasha replied "You know, I love to make love to a young girl! The only trouble is that in the morning, you got to TALK to her!"

A few years ago, Sasha called to ask if he could come to a rehearsal of the NY Chamber Symphony at the 92nd St. Y in order to say hello to Bela Davidovitch, our piano soloist, whom he had not seen in many years. I was happy to oblige, and after Madame Davidovitch had finished rehearsing, I brought Sasha to where she sat in the auditorium. They greeted each other warmly, after which Ms. Davidovitch introduced Sasha to a lady who was sitting with her. The lady remarked that she and Sasha had met many years before. "Ja?" said Sasha, "did ve make lov?"

Catherine Cot:

I started to really know Sasha after my mother died. He was a good friend of my parents since the 2nd World War when they were exiled in the U.S. When he passed through Paris he would stay with them in the Ile St. Louis and the great room was "Sasha's room". I remember my mother telling me about holidays spent with Sasha in our house on the Lac d'Annecy with Dora Maar (one of Picasso's wives) doing the dishes and Sasha playing the "fiddle" to accompany her.

In 1985, a few months after my mother's death, I went to visit him in Paradou and since then I spent each year a few days with him there. The last summer (91) we spent together he would turn his back to the garden saying "I don't want to see all this beauty I will soon leave." The day he died, I sent him a drawing of him turning his back to the garden and hoping to come visit him soon in New York. The souvenirs I have must be common to his friends who came to Paradou: his ritual walk along the new golf course, angry because it ruined the countryside, the market at Arles, his friend Jean–Pierre, his presenting me as his new wife, the meticulous choosing of fresh goat cheese etc... He had many friends in the area and maybe something (a concert?) should be done in his house there.

During the summer of 91 I made a small interview with him for a magazine. He kept saying that all he had to say was in his book, but to hear his voice, his "Americano–Lithuanian–Jewish" accent in speaking French, keeps him present.

It is difficult for me to tell you about any specific moment. We had a very passionate relationship, a mixture of tenderness and fights. He would lose his temper, so would I, he would regret and offer me presents, so would I. With him I forgot I was with an old man and I am grateful to him for everything he brought and taught me. His art of living, independence, generosity, frankness.

Please excuse my poor English (about as bad punctuation as Sasha's).

I hope his paintings and furniture are bought by real friends and that his "batik" goes to a museum as he wished.

Rene A. Morel:

Sasha always was anxious to show me and especially to test me on his cooking, which he claimed was very special.

After many invitations to meet him at his place in the south of France, in the town of Paradou, I finally made it in the summer of 1987. He was very happy to show me his place and the town. The next day he took me to the food market in Arles. He was driving a small Renault car. At 60 km an hour on the highway everyone was passing him. He cursed them and asked why are they in so much of a hurry. "All of those Schmoekedores!" In the market every merchant knew him. They called him Maitre Schneider. The special he was to impress me with, we had to get at the fish stand. In there he purchased some special red fishes of a fairly small size, very famous in the Mediterranean Sea.

On the way back we stopped the car along a small country road, picking rosemary and all sorts of seasoning herbs. Reaching home he took a flat baking pan, put the herbs in it, added a little bit of oil and the red fish with some mussels. He cooked all of these in the same way we purchased them, without emptying or cleaning the insides. And this was, in his opinion, the very best way to cook fish. He noticed that I was not too excited about his haute cuisine and for that he opened another bottle of wine. I had a great time being with him alone for a few days. And that will stay with my best of Sasha memories.

Itzhak Perlman:

In London a few years ago, Sasha, my wife Toby, and I, went to dinner at a wonderful Chinese restaurant. I think we ordered everything on the menu, and the table was overflowing with the many dishes they brought. Eventually Toby and I had eaten our fill, and there were still dishes we had hardly sampled. However, Sasha never stopped! He ate and ate, and we were incredulous at the amount of food he was consuming. Eventually, when he had eaten everything on the table, we left the restaurant and took a taxi. In the taxi, Sasha began complaining of a terrible stomach ache. He was soon in agony. I asked him why he had eaten such an inordinate amount of food. Between monumental groans, he replied that from the days of his childhood, living in very poor circumstances, he had been taught to finish every bit of food served, and not to leave even a morsel. It became his habit of a lifetime.

Karen Elaine Sanders:

I was a viola section player in the winter of 1985 (4th chair viola).

Sasha's emphatic cry "Rrrr–tm, Rrrr–tm, you children play with no Rrrr–tm!!!" is something I find myself telling my own students now (sometimes even lapsing into the Maestro's accent pronouncing "Rhythm" without the "th"!).

The one season I was privileged to perform in the group has left an indelible mark on my love for him and music.

Lisa Seischab:

In November of 1988, I was chosen to participate in the New York String Orchestra Seminar as principal bassoonist. I eagerly awaited the eleven day program, which would be highlighted by performances at Carnegie Hall and the Kennedy Center.

My excitement quickly turned to anxiety a few minutes into the first rehearsal, as conductor Alexander Schneider indicated his extreme displeasure with my bland interpretation of Mozart's *Symphony No. 33*. From that point on, the orchestra was constantly, often vehemently urged to give more, to take care that each note and phrase was given the energy and emotion it deserved.

My need for a new bassoon was clearly evident, as Sasha constantly reminded me (sometimes more earnestly than others!) that my Fox student model couldn't provide the volume he wanted. I'm sure that the rest of the orchestra would have been willing to start a "New Instrument Fund" for me by the end of the seminar just so they wouldn't have to hear him comment on it one more time!

The busy rehearsal schedule, combined with the exertion required at each, left me exhausted, but I quickly managed to revive each time our 80 year old Maestro took to the podium. His commitment to our perfection outweighed any signs of his own fatigue.

It is our final concert on December 29 that I remember most fondly. Our interpretation of Mozart's *Symphony No. 33*, *Piano Concerto No. 12* and *Serenade No. 9* had been painstakingly molded in our eleven days together, and the precise acoustics of the Carnegie Hall stage served to further magnify the success of our performance.

My memory of the 80–year–old Schneider leading this orchestra of 15–22 year–olds will always be very moving to me. His enthusiastic desire for us to carry the orchestral tradition into the future was an inspiration. When my exuberance as a concert–goer or performer begins to wane, these events and lessons in my memory help to place me back on course.

Stephen Burns:

Joy and sadness fill my heart as my appreciation overflows when I think of Sasha. I remain forever changed after our angst filled rehearsals and euphoric performances followed by unbridled celebrations of Music & Life.

The image of Sasha in his devil–horned hat, dancing Strauss waltzes to the accompaniment of, dare I say it – 4 trumpets!!! Even the brasses have been touched by this generous genius beseeching us to listen and express the richness of every note

Selma Klein:

It was at a concert at Carnegie Hall, I was seated behind Alexander Schneider. Kathleen Battle was the soloist before the symphony. I turned to my friend and said, "I can hear her but I wish I could really see her." Sasha was seated in the first row of the mezzanine in an aisle seat. He turned to me and quietly suggested we change seats. I never forgot it.

Isador Saslav:

Ann and I saw Sasha as recently as last season when he conducted the Fort Worth Chamber Orchestra at Texas Christian University. (Was that a proper place for a nice Jewish boy like him to conduct?) We were told by regular fans of that orchestra that no one had ever made them sound so full and rich. That sounds about right; Sasha never was one to let string players sit back and relax while he could keep a suspicious eye on them. We went out afterwards with him to a reception and during our conversation he told us about his contraband, unpublishable memoirs and promised to send us a copy. When we received the thick volume in its plain grey covers and read through it we understood why the outspoken AS could find no willing libel–suit proof publishers.

Further along in our Fort Worth conversation we discovered that despite some 20 years having had time to go by, Sasha had never forgiven me for being a coeditor at the Joseph Haydn Institute in Cologne, helping to edit the complete string quartets for the Henle Edition. I still remember our first conversation on the subject sometime in the early 70's backstage in Puerto Rico at the Casals Festival. Sasha's reaction when discovering the fact of my recent appointment as coeditor was: "What! I've been playing these quartets all my life and now *you're* going to tell me how to play them!"

Besides the festivals in Puerto Rico I participated in the "traveling Sasha Schneider Festival" as imported into the Twin Cities of Minneapolis–St. Paul by Ted Ptashne when I was the Minneapolis Symphony concertmaster. Ted was so very proud to have brought Sasha to his home town and to be able to act as his assistant concertmaster for once.

Like so many others I remember Sasha's parties on 20th Street and his showing off on his violin with its amplifying "his–master's–voice" horn. I once greeted him in NY and he announced that I had come on a special day: his birthday! Of course, as I later discovered, this was one of 365 birthdays he liked to celebrate each year.

Richard Fredrickson:

The first time I worked with Sasha was at the Casals Festival in Puerto Rico in 1972. I was very young then, and Sasha's brusque manner was a great shock until one got used to it. I remember his stopping during the first rehearsal and, looking very put upon, shouting at the violins "Vy you doing dat? You know I don't like dat! Vat are you doink to me?"

Later in the Festival, we were rehearsing Casals' El Pessebre with the chorus. Sasha was trying to get the chorus to make a certain sound, and, not being successful, finally in exasperation, shouted "Don' sqveeze de troat (throat), don sqveeze de troat!" The musicians were doubled over trying to hide their laughter, for Sasha's favorite admonition was always "Don sqveeze de bow!"

Back side of Sasha's 50th birthday party announcement.

And who can ever forget him screaming at the top of his voice, "RE–LAX!" which always made everyone more tense than before. Sasha was one of the true originals in the world of music, and I will never forget him.

Henry Hutchinson:

When Loren asked if I could contribute any particular reminiscences about Sasha, I drew a complete blank, although I felt I must have stored many specific memories somewhere in my head. Then one day when we were rehearsing the Beethoven 9th, (I am the concertmaster of the Puerto Rico Symphony and we use the same parts that were used in the early Casals Festivals), I turned a page in the last movement, and there, as big as life, in Sasha's inimitable handwriting, was his admonition to himself: "Schmoekedores, off!" I started to laugh, as I recalled the many times he screamed similar imprecations at us in his years with the Festival. What warm memories, and sadness too, at the loss of this great artist and grand personality.

Elana Fremerman:

I had the great fortune to play in the 1991 New York String Orchestra as a violist, the first and only time I got to work under Mr. Schneider. I spent the whole ten days or so in the back of the viola section, soaking him in. Unfortunately from where I was sitting, his ferocious podium stomping and shrieking was more distant than I would have liked. In some ways, the wild, frenetic atmosphere that permeated the first few stands of each section dissipated slightly by the time it reached us. Even so, I enjoyed the experience, of course Sasha never singled out my stand partner or me or spoke to us individually.

At his party after the last Carnegie concert, I did get to say hello (actually, it was good–bye). As the party was winding down and I was going home, I wanted to say good–bye and thank–you to Mr. Schneider. He was sitting on the couch in the back of his living room flanked by Rosemary and Frank Salomon. Rosemary realized I was trying to get his attention to say good–bye and said, "Sasha, I think someone would like to say good–bye to you." Then he stopped talking (to Joshua Bell, I think, who was sitting to his right and who I was already feeling sheepish around, as most 21–year–old female string players might be inclined to) and he peered up at me.

I said thank–you for everything, or something like that, and he indicated that I should lean over to give him a quick hug good–bye. As I straightened back up he said to me in his wonderfully thick accent: "Remembuh! I am AVAILABLE!" and then resumed his conversation. I won't forget it and it certainly gave me something to remember him by. (Also with your letter, I found out for the first time that Sasha and I shared the same birthday, October 21, albeit 62 years between us).

101

Barbara Lilly:

Sasha and Mischa stopped by several times — always, it seemed, when we had company. On one of those nights, Sasha asked about my job (I was a copywriter at a local ad agency) and I described my accounts, one of which was the East Ohio Gas Company in Cleveland. "I'll make a commercial for you," he said. And a couple of weeks later I received a record (this was the pre–tape era) which Sasha describes in the following excerpt from his book:

This reminds me of another very funny experience. When advertising on radio and television was in the teen-ages, I had a part–time secretary who also worked for an advertising agency. One day, I asked her to tell me what she was doing at her job and she told me that the Cleveland Gas Company, one of their clients, wanted a good advertisement for the radio and was offering $500 if accepted and if refused, $25 as compensation for the effort. I said, "Let me see what I may be able to do." She laughed, but anyway I did the following. Being on very friendly terms with Columbia Records I made the following recording which, of course, had to be only one minute long! I had my fiddle ready and started by saying, "Listen, when I was a kid in Vilna it was so cold I couldn't play the fiddle, but now by using Cleveland Gas Company gas for heating, my hands are so warm that I can play very fast – so fast that even George Szell wants me in the Cleveland Orchestra!" and then I played very fast a famous Kruetzer etude. I delivered it to my secretary who took it to the company. The result – refused, not good enough – and a check for $25. I think today I would make a lot of money with it and if I'm not mistaken, Isaac Stern has the record. I certainly hope Itzhak Perlman gets paid more for his advertisements!

I think Sasha did get paid $25, though I doubt the gas company was offering $500 for a commercial; writing them was part of my job. I tried in the past to track down the record and hope Isaac Stern — or someone — has it. I'd kill for a copy.

I saw Sasha last about 2 or 3 years ago. He had aged. But then, so have I. Sad though I am at his death, the thought of him brings a smile to my lips.

Dmitry Kristanovich:

I have a particularly fond memory of Mr. Schneider during the 1991 String Seminar in New York. It was about halfway through the seminar, and by this time, I had gotten a feel for what working with Mr. Schneider was like.

During rehearsals, Mr. Schneider always had a great way of bringing across his ideas to everyone in the orchestra. Whenever he demonstrated something by playing it on his violin, it was always easy to understand what he had in mind. Although he might not have played a figure with polish, it didn't matter because the content of what he was expressing was always clear.

One night after dinner, I was the first to come back to the rehearsal room, and I walked in on Mr. Schneider practicing. He was playing the 24th Paganini Caprice, and it sounded incredible. The beauty, style, and control of those few seconds that I heard were truly breathtaking. Upon seeing me, Mr. Schneider quickly stopped playing, and put away his violin, almost as if embarrassed. He sat down on his conducting chair and started going through the pages of a piece that the orchestra was playing, as if he'd never been playing at all.

This was very touching and his modesty for what he was doing was surprising. Mr. Schneider was one of the most special people I've met and I think that there are not enough words to describe his contributions to music.

Isador Saslav:

Knowing how much Sasha did for the performance of Vivaldi's works I was always amused by one happening at the Festival Casals. Often displaying an impatience with the harpsichord in Vivaldi's music, Sasha on this occasion substituted a piano. But of course he must have suspected that what was coming out was not quite authentic so he kept shushing the piano up on try after try. Finally, only when the piano became completely inaudible and was performing a sort of pantomimic accompaniment to the strings was Sasha finally satisfied. The keyboard was visually present for the sake of authenticity but Sasha was not about to let its actual sounds interfere with the music supplied by the strings!

Sasha, when faced with a tonal problem with the corps under his leadership would get up and imprecate us with: *"DUN'T SQVEEZE DE BOW!"* Thus was I afforded an invaluable key to bowing technique on the violin: "HOLD THE BOW BUT DUN'T SQVEEZE IT!"

David Wallace:

Being principal violist for Sasha's final string seminar was and will remain one of the most memorable musical experiences of my life. Of the numerous anecdotes I could write, one particularly comes to mind. During one rehearsal, Mr. Schneider stood scolding the orchestra (as only Sasha could), when his voice cracked. He sat down, fingered his throat, and mumbled, "My God, I can't scream anymore!"

Rarely has screaming ever been so inspirational!

Mayuki Fukuhara:

In the Brandenburg Ensemble tour bus, he asked me if I was Jewish. To my uncertain answer he said, "You mishugana!" and left to go prey on the next victim.

"Phrase it!" on the Carnegie Hall stage. He stopped the orchestra and said, "Can't you phrase it! Mark it!" We try again, then silence. Raged conductor glaring around at the kids. I thought, "... I phrased, who didn't and looked around." Both of our eyes met. Now he was staring at me, then he came over to my stand, looked into my part, what he found was a mark which only my stand partner and I would play it with artistic nuance. He grabbed a pencil, drew the powerful mark of crescendo and said, "You have to mark it!" Young man's hot blood went up to his head. But!! he thought, "Mr. S. knows much, much more than me." Then every thing was fine. I had one of the greatest sessions in my life. At the final reception, I asked him, "You told us to scratch, but isn't it better to give just the right amount of bow pressure?" He looked at me and started laughing with Mr. Laredo who said "I will make him scratch!" Then he warmly said "At my age, even I don't want scratch!"

I thought "This is a place that only the best players come to. How could I fit in? What am I doing here...?" A little later I saw my first rehearsal on the schedule board (Brahms Sextet in Bb Major). I went into the rehearsal room with some fear. There he was, already practicing. Then with a warm expression on his face, he turned and looked and said "Oh, how are you?" I closed my eyes and played, answering to what I heard. It was one of the most beautiful memories in my life.

He said "Today, all over the world, people play with their head, but not their heart." I will always remember the rehearsals and performance of the Haydn Symphony w/ four horns. So spirited. It truly went up there and it was definitely his singing.

105

A moment of contemplation before a concert. Photo: T. Suárez

Anna Malkin:

There are so many memories that I could talk about when it comes to Sasha. He was, without a doubt, the strongest influence for me in terms of music and how it affects my life. He gave me the opportunity that I never thought I could have; my chance to solo at Carnegie Hall.

I have never in my life enjoyed and loved music as I did when I participated in the 1992 New York String Orchestra. Not only did Sasha make the music such a big part of him, but he made it a part of us. Every note had to be just perfect.

He would tell us the funniest stories, like how he heard the Bach Concerto (in c minor for violin and oboe) played

106

by two harpsichords. The story itself wasn't so funny, but the way he told it, I'll never forget. He started by telling us that he heard it on the radio the night after I had played it. He said that they played it so fast and so bad. Then he said "You can't play doodle, doodle, doodle and tiki, tiki, taki. Articulate!!!!" The latter was one of the words he said to us a hundred times every day. And he would pronounce every syllable just to make his point.

I never anticipated his death. I knew that he was eighty–four and he had had a heart attack, but he had so much energy. Sometimes, I could have sworn that he had more energy than we did. Once, he wanted to show us a particular bow stroke in the Bach, so he gripped my arm. I thought my arm was going to fall off! He had the strongest grip. Also, he would stomp his feet on the podium and yell at us. That's not to say he was a mean person. On the contrary.

During the days of the seminar, Sasha and I grew very close. We spent lots of time talking between rehearsals. I think I was a sort of link to his past because I spoke Russian. For a man of 84, he spoke impeccably. He would even talk to me in Russian in front of the whole orchestra as if I didn't speak English. He would tell me lots of stories, but most of all he loved to talk to me about music. We shared musical ideas about certain phrasings, tempos, etc.

I remember after the first rehearsal at Carnegie, he told me and my father, whom he respected and admired both as a person and as a teacher, that the members of the orchestra were lazy and that we had no discipline. The more I thought about it, the more I realized that what he said was the truth.

I can't speak for other members, but I can tell you what Sasha did for me.

Before the seminar, I didn't know if I even wanted to continue playing the violin. I was confused about what I wanted to do with my life. Sasha changed all of that by showing me what music was really about. It wasn't just notes, or playing all the dynamics on the page. He told me, "You

107

must play from your heart so that every note means something to you." After the seminar, I wanted to practice and give music a shot. Who knows, if I keep practicing, maybe someday I'll play in Carnegie Hall again. But sadly, Sasha won't be there to share it with me.

Sasha was convinced that I was related to his first teacher, who was a Malkin. He told everyone that I had great blood from both sides of my family. I think he was right. We know for sure that Jascha Heifetz was a close cousin on my mom's side and on my dad's, well maybe Sasha really knew. We don't know anything about my dad's side of the family because his father died when my dad was a year and a half. I told this to Sasha, but he kept insisting that I was related.

Before the Christmas Eve concert, I went to ask Sasha a detail question. When I walked into his dressing room, he asked me if I had a room. I was so shocked. I didn't know that I would get my own. Well, he yelled at a lady who was supposed to have given me one and it was so funny that I forgot to ask my question.

Anyway, after the concert, I thanked Sasha for the room, but most of all for giving me the chance to solo at Carnegie Hall. He didn't even want to accept thanks. He said that it was my hard work, not his that got me on the stage. Somehow, I just don't believe that. If it wasn't for him, I don't think I would even want to consider music anymore. I would also never play on that stage.

Sasha opened up a whole new world for me. He made my dreams come true and I'm glad I got to tell him that before he died. But, I wish I could've said good–bye. I'm so lucky to have known him and to have played with him. He is and always will be a legend, in my book anyway.

80th birthday party invitation.

Please come to my 80ᴿ Birthday
5 East - 20ᴿ St. N.Y.C.
October 21ˢᵗ 11 P.M.

COLOR FIGUERES

Sasha .

Text of 80th birthday party invitation.

Alexandra Maria Tsilibes:

As I was preparing to audition for Mr. Schneider, I could not help but think how wonderful it would be to be a part of next year's orchestra, the 25th New York String Orchestra — what a celebration it would be. But how lucky I was to make the 1992 orchestra, the 24th and Mr. Schneider's last. You cannot imagine how it felt to be on the stage of Carnegie Hall on December 24th at midnight on my 20th birthday. What a way to start a new year and a new decade, making music at Carnegie Hall with Sasha! This I will never forget as long as I live — to work with one of the legends of music, to experience a connection with the grand tradition of string playing.

Yes, there will be a very special celebration on the 24th of December 1993 at midnight, but somewhere way up high. And when Sasha raises his baton to lead his celestial band of string players at the pearly gates in a Johann Strauss Waltz, I too, will raise my birthday glass of fine champagne and say, "Thank you, Sasha."

110

Jeffrey S. Borer, M.D.

I was privileged to know Sasha for only a little over a year before he died. After I had seen him in my office several times (and watched him at the end of each visit walk around the office to say good–bye to the various doctors, administrators and secretaries—especially the women) he brought me a gift: two of his record albums. In the first, relatively more recent, effort, he conducted the Chamber Orchestra of Europe. In the second, a reissue, he played with the Budapest String Quartet in pieces recorded between 1932 and 1936. When he gave me the second he said, "This one you surely have never seen!" However, when I looked at the album cover, I was startled to realize that, indeed, I had the album and, until that moment, it had never occurred to me that the famous 84 year old musician I was seeing was the same Schneider whose picture, as an already adult performer, stared out among the four musicians photographed at work 60 years before. Any doubt as to identity was dispelled on April 19, when Sasha invited my wife, my two children and me to hear his annual and, it turned out, last performance of Haydn's "The Seven Last Words..." He had been released from the hospital only a few days before and his frailty and fatigue, together with failing eyesight and hearing, were known to few in the auditorium—and to none from the glorious rendition that ensued. The intense feeling, color and shading and precision of his play belied his physical condition and stood well with the superb play on the old record. To understand this awesome capacity, I read his privately published autobiography (another gift) which indicated the enthusiasm and spirit which Sasha clearly brought to all his involvements, and explains how such outward verve could persist even to the end. He was truly a giant!

Suzanne M. Forman:

Stan and I were new friends of Sasha. We met him a few weeks before he died, on the occasion of a concert he was conducting at the New School.

We were touched by his vigor and enthusiasm and by the rapport and harmony with his orchestra. We felt so lucky to have discovered him and vowed to become regulars at his New School performances.

After the wine and cheese reception, we strolled on the way home with no particular route in mind. I looked across the street and recognized Sasha being helped out of a car. There was so much pain in his face and he appeared to be expressing the pain to his companion who helped him to the door of the building.

Very shortly after this incident, I read about his death. We are so sad that we were not able to get to know him better, and extend our sincere sympathy to his family and close friends.

Homer Mensch:

Sasha and I had a special relationship. He used my students in every one of his string seminars – and many of these players are now first chairs of major symphony orchestras. They loved him so much and learned what it meant to accomplish a great deal in a very short period of time during those Christmas holidays. I will miss him as I know these young bass players will also. He was truly a good friend and a *mensch*.

Sasha, double bass virtuoso. Photo: T. Suárez.

Reed Smith:

My favorite recollection of my two years in his Christmas String Seminar is of going to his apartment after the New Years Eve concert, rolling back the oriental rugs and dancing to Strauss waltzes until the wee hours of the morning.

His gift to hundreds, probably thousands of young musicians demonstrated his rare qualities.

Lily West:

I knew Sasha for forty years: for two or three of those years as a casual acquaintance, and then, increasingly, as a dear friend. What instantly struck me about him – and seemed, throughout our acquaintance, a salient feature of his personality – was his apparently limitless capacity for enthusiasm and energy: attributes which in Sasha's case seemed combined; two parts of a compound whole.

He was one of those fortunate people whose enthusiasm is readily kindled by a vast array of beloved delights. For Sasha, this array included almost every pleasurable perception available to any of the senses – from music making to cooking to every agreeable kind of human intercourse from sex to jokes to talks and walks; to the visual delights of landscape and architecture, painting and drawing, colors and textures in clothes, in a room; to languages and a widely ranging appetite for reading and talking about books written in English, or French, or German, or Russian. And his ability to transmit this sense of enthusiasm to others was as vigorous as the enthusiasm itself. Anyone listening to him make music or talk, or watching him cook, stirring, tasting and sniffing con amore – or even walk, with a rapid, eager spring more like a run than a walk – could not fail to be aware of the fact that he thought what he was doing was Great! – if and when that was the case: which it was, much of the time.

114

I had a sad good fortune (not a contradiction in terms, but how it actually was) of seeing a great deal of Sasha during the summer of 1992: the last summer of his life. He had come back from France quite ill, and when he left the hospital, he went home to his house on 20th Street accompanied by a resident nurse. The nurse, a warmhearted person, prepared to accommodate the ornery whims of difficult patients, clearly appreciated Sasha and enjoyed exchanging banter and jokes. "He's easy enough to get on with", she said to me. (A judgment which may startle the legions of people exposed to the impatient, flaring temper which was an intrinsic part of any extended give and take with Sasha). "All you have to do," she said, "is pay him no mind when he talks mean".

During the month of August, most of Sasha's friends and acquaintances were out of town. I was not only in town, but lived at the other end of a short walk from 20th Street. That being so, I walked over to see him most afternoons. He (and the nurse) both seemed to appreciate visits; a punctuation point in the day.

The point of this recollection, however, is that even in those circumstances, when he was feeling physically pretty wiped out, and spiritually, very downhearted about his situation and prospects – even in those dire circumstances – his enthusiasm, including the desire to communicate and transmit it – was still present. In this case that quality focused – for much of my visits – on my efforts to attain spoken fluency in Russian. We conversed in Russian about this and that – and my failings of intonation and accent aroused Sasha's didactic impulse. He undertook to improve and polish my performance ; an effort he seemed to find diverting – until his patience ran out: how soon that happened varied from day to day, and depended, among other things, on the state of his energy and physical comfort at the time. (His failing heart was the source of pretty constant discomfort). Nonetheless, part of each visit consisted of my reading aloud, in Russian, a piece of Chekhov's story *The Lady with a Little Dog*, and receiving a running critical commentary as I went along: critical attention which extended beyond my reading to the story itself.

"It's a terrific story," Sasha said, "but I think it would be better without the first paragraph". And if Chekhov himself had been present, Sasha would certainly have told him.

Arlene Gould:

The Christmas Eve concert of 1992 was the last time I saw Sasha. He looked frail but he somehow got that orchestra to sparkle and sing. He was tired back stage after the concert and I'm not even sure he knew who I was. But as always, he gave me a big hug and said he was glad I'd come. Last February 3rd when I heard about his death, I was shocked and absolutely grief stricken. Somehow I just wasn't prepared for him not to still be around. I'll always think of him as my musical father. I still see him clearly whenever I hear Brandenburg #3.

Loren Glickman:

The last time Sasha and I were together was about a month or two before he died. Dobbie and I took him to a nice restaurant, and he was relaxed and enjoying the food and the conversation. But no matter what the subject, somehow Sasha managed to shift the emphasis to providing for the musical education of young people. We were discussing the depressed value of real estate. Sasha said "My building is worth three million dollars in a better market. You can buy it for $300,000.! Then I could have that much money to leave to the kids."

Since we no longer worked together, Sasha did not really know much about my present way of life. During the same dinner, he asked "Are you still playing the bassoon?" Taken aback, I replied "Certainly!" "Vy" he persisted. "Why, why – –" I stuttered, "because that is what I do best, because I love performing, and I still play well." Sasha countered "You should stop playing and let the young people have your jobs!"

Sasha with Loren Glickman. December, 1992. Photo: Dobbie Glickman.

117

Frank E. Taplin, Jr.:

Sasha — the irrepressible, the irreplaceable, lover of wine, women, and song (in no particular order) — was graced by the Gods with a passion and a joy in life that were highly contagious and made the world a happier place. How well we recall his work with young musicians at Marlboro, his Carnegie Hall Christmas concerts, his work with Pablo Casals and Rudolf Serkin, his Budapest Quartet years, his encouragement of the Guarneri Quartet and so many others.

Once, after a Marlboro Music concert in Princeton, Peg and I (in absentia) gave Sasha and his friends a post–concert party in our home. We were in London at the time. During the evening the telephone rang. It was Sasha, calling collect, to say that he was enjoying our Chateau Palmer wine to the full. Pure Sasha!

My memories of him are so vivid, and my regret is that we did not visit him in southern France, as he had urged us to do, at his paradise in Paradou.

Here is my telegram to Sasha on his 60th birthday:

> Favorite food – potatoes masha,
> Favorite house – a Vilna dacha,
> Favorite music – lots of pasha,
> Played by incredible favorite – Sasha.

CODA
Loren Glickman

To try to define the essence of Sasha Schneider's life in its simplest terms, I would choose the word passion. Try to think, of all your acquaintances, of anyone else who really lived so passionately in every aspect of his life. Sasha exuded passion in his music, in everyday conversation, in friendship, and, naturally, in love. There was never any subterfuge, any connivance, any subtle gamesmanship. No. It was always truth, direct, out front. Take it or leave it! Arguments with him could be devastating but <u>he</u> was never devastated, only <u>honest</u>.

Sometimes drastic decisions were made on a moment's notice. Everyone connected would be horrified. Not Sasha! I recall a particular occasion: A musician who had played in all of Sasha's orchestras of the fifties and sixties, a man whom Sasha had known in his early years in Germany and who had been a guest in Sasha's house countless times, ventured an opinion at a large party, to the effect that Isaac Stern was an overrated solo artist. In a flash, Sasha jumped up, screamed imprecations at the man, threw him out of his house and told him never to return! Some days later, when Sasha was quite sober, I suggested that he talk to the musician, and say that possibly his actions had been somewhat overbearing, considering their friendship going back forty years. Sasha's response was just as vehement as on the night of the party: "What right does a musician of such moderate ability have, to pass judgment on an artist as great as Isaac? And in my house, no less! No, I will never talk to him again!"

Israel was his passion, Casals was his passion, music, women, food, friendship – all were his passions. But the greatest of all, in the last twenty–five years of his life, was his passion for the musical development of "the young people." No conversation on any subject lasted ten minutes without Sasha making reference to young musicians and

119

what could be done to help them. Is it any wonder that we read in those letters from "the young people" such emotional outpourings of love and appreciation for their good fortune in having been the recipients of his love and passionate dedication to their musical education?

What a legacy he left us! Hundreds of musicians all over the world will vibrantly remember Sasha Schneider, and their whole lives will continue to be enriched by his never–fading memory.

What a legacy he left us!

FINE

Sasha with student orchestra. Photo: T. Suárez.

Alexander Schneider 1908-1993

The small Russian city of Vilna produced both Jascha Heifetz and Alexander Schneider. Heifetz went on to become the world's greatest solo violinist, and Schneider achieved renown as a chamber musician, a solo artist, a symphony conductor and as the organizer of festivals the world over.

Alexander (or Sasha) began earning his living as a violinist at an early age. He played in the streets, in cafes and even in bordellos. At 16 he went to Frankfurt to study at the Hochschum Conservatory and played in the Frankfurt Symphony. At age 19 he was appointed Concertmaster of the Norddeutscher Rundfunk in Hamburg. However, with Hitler's rise to power, Schneider, a Jew, was asked to leave the orchestra. By pure chance the Budapest String Quartet had a vacancy on the second violin chair; Schneider auditioned and was accepted. The relationship lasted for forty-five years.

The quartet settled in Paris but toured the world. By 1938 it was lauded as the finest in the world; recorded for Columbia Records and was booked solid year round. In 1939 it was invited to be resident string quartet at the Library of Congress in Washington, where it remained almost 25 years.

Schneider left the Quartet in 1944 and soon after organized the New York Piano Quartet and the Albeneri Trio. He performed recitals with the harpsichordist Ralph Kirkpatrick, directed chamber music concerts at Dumbarton Oaks in Washington and performed solo recitals at the Library of Congress. In the summers, he taught at Washington State University in Seattle.

In 1947 he became an American citizen, grateful for having been accepted by this country and not suffering the fate of his mother and sister, both of whom died at Auschwitz.

Schneider first played for the great cellist and humanitarian, Pablo Casals, in 1947. The next year he studied the unaccompanied Bach Suites with Casals and subsequently performed them in solo recitals worldwide. He considered Casals, Diran Alexanian (cellist) and Artur Schnabel, the great romantic pianist, as artists with the strongest influence on his own development. He played chamber music with all three and attributed to these experiences his maturing artistry, freedom of expression and musical fantasy.

Schneider was instrumental in organizing the first Casals Festival in Prades in 1950. The Haydn Society asked him to organize the Schneider Quartet and perform all of Haydn's string quartets in 21

121

concerts and to record them. Funding ran out before the project was completed, but the concerts were highly acclaimed.

In 1956 he was asked to rejoin the Budapest String Quartet. He did so with the understanding that he could also continue his widening musical interests. The group was thus reunited to the satisfaction of chamber music lovers worldwide.

While browsing through the music stacks at the Library of Congress, Schneider discovered the waltzes and ländler of Josef Lanner and fell in love with them, declaring them the equal of those of Johann Strauss. He performed them with such warmth, style and panache that audiences were captivated. Columbia Records recorded an album of Schneider leading a small ensemble in these Viennese delights.

In the 1950's he inaugurated a series of concerts at Circle in the Square, and in 1953 a series of free chamber music concerts in Washington Square Park in New York City. He started an annual Christmas Eve midnight concert in Carnegie Hall. Tickets were inexpensive and difficult to obtain. The New School for Social Research invited him to direct a series of chamber concerts and he accepted with the proviso that tickets would cost no more than one dollar. He remained artistic director until his death in 1993.

In 1955 he joined the faculty of the Marlboro School of Music, functioning in the summertime under the direction of Rudolf Serkin. He spent the next 20 summers there and one year took the Marlboro orchestra on a world concert tour.

Schneider was instrumental in advancing the careers of many young soloists, including Peter Serkin, Murray Perahia, Ani and Ida Kavafian, Richard Stolzman, Pinchas Zukerman and Shlomo Mintz. Although most people identify Schneider with baroque music, Mozart and Schubert, he performed many works by contemporary composers, including music of Foss, Sessions, Kirchner, Babbitt, Berio and Krenek, as well as Stravinsky, Villa-Lobos, Bartok, Berg and Copland.

In 1957, the Government of Puerto Rico, wishing to honor Pablo Casals, whose mother had been born in Puerto Rico, asked Schneider to put together a festival of international stature. He accomplished this with such success that in one year the festival achieved international acclaim. For the next 20 years Schneider maintained the high quality of the Festival Casals, performing concerts not only in Puerto Rico but in Mexico, San Salvador, Venezuela, The Dominican Republic, New York's Carnegie Hall and at The United Nations. In addition to the Festivals he helped found the Puerto Rico

122

Conservatory of Music and the Puerto Rico Symphony. He hoped gifted young Puerto Rican musicians would achieve professional stature at the Conservatory and move on to the Symphony. This came to pass and the Puerto Rico Symphony is now a fine orchestra, comparable with many in the United States and Europe.

Alexander Schneider made his first trip to Israel with the Budapest Quartet in 1959. Playing in kibbutzim as well as principal cities, he was so impressed by the pioneer spirit of the people that he resolved to lend support to the artistic communities in Israel. He helped organize the first music festival and brought great chamber music and the finest solo artists to participate. He returned almost every year, always taking the programs into the hinterlands.

During those years, he bought a second house in Provence, France, and used it as refuge from his normal hectic routine. Here he could relax from the pressure of work. Yet even here, he managed to organize a chamber orchestra of the best players in Paris and gave baroque concerts both in Paris and in Menton.

In 1961 President Kennedy invited Pablo Casals, Alexander Schneider and Mieczyslaw Horszowski to perform a concert of chamber music at the White House, giving the art a tremendous boost and national attention. He later (1966) received a $400,000. grant from the National Endowment Fund to form a National Chamber Orchestra. He traveled all over the country listening to some 600 applicants for this 40 member ensemble. There was great excitement in musical circles and even players from great American symphonies auditioned in the hope of being accepted into this "dream orchestra" Unfortunately, opposition from the managements of the best known symphony orchestras, who wanted the funds directed to established orchestras, ultimately prevented the successful outcome of the project, much to Schneider's disappointment.

In 1967 the Budapest Quartet disbanded because of members' illnesses. The artists had been together so long that rather than carry on playing trios or replacing ailing members, they decided to leave the field while still recognized as the best quartet in the world. Schneider then moved to New York. He loved to cook and entertain. His friends included photographers Gjon Mili, Robert Capa and Margaret Bourke-White, painter Saul Steinberg, composers Igor Stravinsky and Vittorio Rieti, performers Isaac Stern and Ralph Kirkpatrick, choreographer George Balanchine and actors Paul Robeson, Zero Mostel, Uta Hagen and Jose Ferrer. He decorated his apartment with works by Matisse, Picasso, Chagall and Calder.

123

The first Christmas Seminar devoted to training gifted young musicians in the Art of Music Performance was in 1969. This project became Schneider's deepest felt enterprise. He loved the "kids" and loved inspiring them to play with greater artistic commitment than ever in their previous experience. Schneider continued this annual event until just a short time before he died. He was so proud of these orchestras! He always contended that no professional orchestra could rival his students in the product of their total commitment.

Alexander Schneider's conducting career continued while he was involved with his other projects. He conducted, among others, the New York Philharmonic, the English Chamber Orchestra, the orchestras of Rio de Janeiro, Costa Rica, the National Orchestra of Greece, the St. Louis Symphony, San Francisco and Dallas Symphonies, the Minnesota Orchestra and the orchestra of the Mostly Mozart Festival.

Alexander Schneider was outspoken, opinionated, even obstreperous. But always *honest* to *his* way of thinking. He wrote his autobiography in 1988 and published it himself rather than have professional editors improve on his language and grammar, soften his statements and generally change the tone of his writing. The book truly gives the reader a compete picture of his passion for music, art, people in general, women in particular, sports, humor, food, drink and LIFE.

L'chayim, Sasha. To life!

Index

125

126